THE EUCHARIST:

DOING WHAT JESUS DID

Frank O'Loughlin

THE EUCHARIST:

DOING WHAT JESUS DID

ST PAULS

THE EUCHARIST:
Doing what Jesus did
© Francis O'Loughlin, 1997

First published, April 1997

National Library of Australia
Cataloguing-in-Publication data:
O'Loughlin, Francis
The Eucharist: doing what Jesus did
Bibliography
ISBN 1 875570 89 6
1. Catholic Church - Doctrines. 2. Lord's Supper -
Catholic Church. I. Title.

234.163

Cover photo: Francisco Rovero's sculpture. Used with permission.

Cover design: Liam Gash, Page and Picture Desktop Design

Printed and bound by Ligare Pty Ltd, Riverwood

Published by
ST PAULS PUBLICATIONS - Society of St Paul,
60-70 Broughton Road - PO Box 906 - Strathfield, NSW 2135

ST PAULS PUBLICATIONS is an activity of the Priests and Brothers of the Society of St Paul who place at the centre of their lives the mission of evangelisation with the means of apostolic communication.

Contents

Introduction

The Catholic approach to the Eucharist in the years since the Council of Trent (1545-1563) has been influenced by the disputes that went on between Catholics and Protestants. Consequently, there has been a strong emphasis on two issues: the real eucharistic presence of Christ, and the Eucharist as a sacrifice. This emphasis predominated until the 1960s. The strength of this polemic caused something of a refraction of the Catholic understanding of the Eucharist which was narrowed down largely to these two aspects which are indeed central but not exhaustive of the theology of the Eucharist.

During this century a deeper appreciation of Catholic tradition has arisen in eucharistic theology, as it has in all branches of theology. This has enabled us:

- to consider the post-Tridentine period within the context of the longer and richer Catholic tradition of two thousand years,
- to gain a richer and broader view of the Eucharist in recent decades when our practice of the Eucharist was undergoing a revitalisation.

The movements which brought about a revival in eucharistic theology were the same movements which have had significant effects in other areas of theology:
- the biblical renewal
- the patristic renewal
- the renewal in the study of the history of theology.

The ecumenical movement added impetus to the common study of things eucharstic between Catholics and Protestants. And obviously the liturgical renewal has had profound effects on our understanding and practice of the Eucharist. In the course of the twentieth century there has been an unprecedented change in the ways of the Church with regard to that which lies at its heart – the Eucharist. I remain convinced that the most important of these was the reform of Pope Pius X which promoted frequent communion for all Catholics. Pius X's documents go back to the first decade of the century. It took some decades to bring about their implementation in the life of the Church, but it brought Catholics to the regular reception of communion for the first time since the patristic age. I believe we are still reaping the harvest of this reform.

Many other reforms have come about since Vatican II with which we are all familiar. This has been not just a change of rites but a change of ritual genre. The pre-Vatican II liturgy had quite different expectations of its participants than those of post-Vatican II liturgy.

The pre-Vatican liturgy was based on a combination of uniformity and individualism. Participants prayed individually in parallel with the liturgical prayer rather than in engagement with it. Uniformity was an almost necessary concomitant to this to maintain the ecclesial character of the prayer. The liturgy, like virtually all others before it, had been unconsciously formed by its cultural environment, a part of which was the high individualism of the age.

The liturgy which has come about as a result of Vatican II and the work issuing from it is of a different genre which asks for a participation of engagement and is deliberately communal or ecclesial in its intentions.

What ultimately lies behind this change is a renewed concept of the Church as the People of God and especially as a communion of life in Christ. This change has come about as the result of a council which was highly conscious that the Church would no longer live in a situation where Christian faith could be taken for granted as a social reality. There would need to be a new deliberateness about our being the Church.

We live at a privileged time in the history of the Church. It is a time of change and transition and one of understandable confusion for many people. Times of social, cultural and religious transition are always difficult and our period of transition is a radical one. Such times are, however, also times of discovery and re-discovery. The abundance of contemporary historical research is enabling us to draw forth old and beautiful things from our tradition. Contemporary perspectives and questions are offering us the possibility to express the same ancient faith within the contours of a new age and culture.

This book represents an attempt at a theology of the Eucharist which takes seriously its status as an *action*. It is an *action* of Christ drawing his disciples into that communion with himself which we call the Church. It is an *action* in which the Church expresses and discovers its own identity which is to be in this communion with Christ.

The book presents the constitutive elements of this *action*:
- Christ's paschal mystery,
- the status of the Eucharist as a memorial *action*,
- our doing what Jesus did in the shape, the symbolic form and the meaning of the *action*,
- the prayer which is constitutive of the *action* – the Eucharistic Prayer.

The treatment of the above elements of eucharistic theology naturally leads on to further elements of eucharistic theology including the important themes of the eucharistic presence of Christ and the Eucharist as sacrifice. (Both aspects are dealt with to some degree in this book but I hope to deal with them more explicitly and at greater length in a further volume, along with other themes of eucharistic theology. Such a volume will deal also with a theology of the reserved Eucharist).

I dedicate this book in particular to the community of the Catholic Church in Melbourne. The Church in that city has been the place where my own faith has been nourished from my earliest years. From that Church and from those of its members closest to me, I have come to recognise Christ in the breaking of the bread. In this I rejoice. I offer this book in the hope that it may enable those who have recognised Christ in the Eucharist to recognise him more deeply, and that it may lead yet others to the same recognition.

1 | *The paschal mystery*

The Eucharist presents itself to us in its rites and texts as giving us access to something beyond itself – the death and resurrection of Jesus Christ which the Christian believes is the source of life for the world. This gives us our identity as Christians. We believe that Jesus died and that he who was dead is not only alive but is the source of life for all. This was the discovery which turned the ragged group of disciples into people who had discovered something beyond all price.

In the Eucharist, the Christian community sees itself as acting in memory of that event. This is expressed in every Eucharistic Prayer just after the Lord's command to repeat what he had done in memory of him. So, in the *Roman Missal*:

The Second Eucharistic Prayer says: 'In memory of his death and resurrection, we offer you, Father this life-giving bread, this saving cup.'

The Third Eucharistic Prayer says: 'Father, calling to mind the death your Son endured... his glorious resurrection... we offer you...'.

The Fourth Eucharistic Prayer says similarly, 'Father, we now celebrate this memorial of our redemption. We recall Christ's death, his resurrection...'.

The ancient *Roman Canon* – the First Eucharistic Prayer - says, 'Father, we celebrate the memory of Christ your Son. We recall his passion, his resurrection from the dead...'.

Each expresses the same rootedness of the Eucharist in Christ's death and resurrection.

The early Church described this death and resurrection of Jesus in terms of the Old Testament terminology of passover. Writers took up this central element of the Jewish faith which gave Judaism its identity and used it to describe what the death and resurrection of Jesus meant for them – the new and definitive passover.

At passover the Jewish people celebrated the exodus of their people out of the slavery of Egypt into the land of freedom and abundance. This involved in its broadest sense, the blood of the lambs smeared on their doorposts in Egypt to save the lives of their first-born sons and so, in their thinking, of their whole people. It involved also leaving the land of slavery to the Egyptians and the false Egyptian idols to go out into the desert on a journey to worship the God of their fathers who called them into the freedom of divine worship. This was a journey of faith asking them to leave behind the false security of idols and to move on, guided by the signs of God's presence, into the land God would give them. It involved the crucial moment in that journey when God made a covenant with them promising to be faithful and asking for their fidelity expressed in obedience to God's word, God's law.

This exodus, this passover, gave Israel its identity. It made them the chosen people of God. Throughout their history they will come back to this event for strength, energy and vision when they enter into crisis.

The early Christians put the death and resurrection of Jesus not only in line with the exodus but in such continuity with it that the Christ-event is given definitive primacy over it, setting off a total reinterpretation of God's history with the people. This is not to disregard the exodus but to see it reaching its fulfilment and to draw it into a new stage of the history of revelation and salvation between God and the chosen people centred now on the person of Christ.

The implication of this alignment is that all that Israel found in the exodus they now can find in new and definitive abundance in Jesus Christ. In his death and resurrection they discover a new passover from slavery to freedom, from death to life, from worship of false idols to the worship of the true God. They discover a new journey of faith based on a covenant with God who is revealed anew in Jesus and in the event of Jesus' death and resurrection.

The implications of this alignment were drawn out slowly. However, from the moment the interaction between Israel's passover and the death and resurrection of Jesus began to occur, they began to discover new meaning, to have new perceptions.

This occurred and continues to occur not just at the level of official theology and texts, but at the level of peoples' religious sensibilities, customs, devotions and feelings. New meaning is discovered in both events: in the Christ-event as perceived in the light of the exodus, and in the exodus in the light of Christ's death and resurrection.

Passover imagery was not the only Old Testament imagery and theology the New Testament used. There was, for example, the imagery of suffering servant, of the saving of Isaac from death, of a new creation. Here we will concentrate upon the passover imagery because it becomes a central thrust in the understanding of the Eucharist and the other sacraments, and indeed in the understanding of the death and resurrection of Jesus as redeeming us. It is also, I believe, a very good form of imagery for us to use in our times. I hope this will become evident as we go along.

'Paschal mystery' is a term which developed as patristic usage out of New Testament perspectives. It has come into prominent use in theology in the course of this century. 'Paschal' refers to 'pasch', the Hebrew word for passover, and the word 'mystery' means not a puzzle but a reality in which human beings find God present and active. For anything to be Christian, it must have a link to the event of Christ's death and resurrection which we consider our passover into God and life. As the first Christians experienced that death and then Christ's presence among them beyond his death, they reached back into their tradition – the life of Israel, the Old Testament and all that derived from it – to find the means to grasp what was going on among them in the life, death and resurrection of Jesus.

The passover of Jesus

We will look at the paschal mystery of Jesus from four points of view corresponding to the way we are used to celebrating it in the liturgical year:
  his death,
  his resurrection,

his ascension or return to the Father,
his sending of the Spirit at Pentecost.

We are not talking about four separate events when we take up these four aspects of the passover of Jesus but rather four aspects or dimensions of his handing over of himself or his return to the Father. We cannot presume to have detailed information about what happens to Jesus in his return to the Father. We use terms like resurrection, return to the Father, glorification, sending of the Spirit on the basis of Old Testament imagery and New Testament developments of that imagery to help us speak about things that we cannot see and hear, and yet things that have been revealed to us in the Christian discovery of the Father's victory over sin and death in God's Son, Jesus Christ.

We also need to avoid a misconception that the spatial nature of our imagery can often suggest, namely, that Jesus' passover is a departure from our world to another world which is, so to speak, somewhere else. Jesus' return to the Father is not a departure from our world into another but the manifestation of his own deepest reality as coming from the Father and returning to the Father. It is in fact the manifestation of the Father's presence in our world for those who have eyes to see, the eyes of faith. The Father and the risen Christ do not dwell in the dimension of our world that we live in, where we know by sight and touch and hearing. But they are of our world at a deeper level than is possible for us. It is theirs in a way that it cannot be ours. They are more intimate to us and to our world than we are to ourselves or our world.

The death and resurrection of Jesus reveals the preciousness of our world to God and God's depth of involvement in it. The world becomes new, different once we see the meaning of Jesus' death and resurrection as an act of the Father who created all things out of nothing. It even reveals to us what evil and death are in God's world once we see them in the perspective of the Father giving us Jesus and taking us to himself in Jesus.

The death of Jesus, as distinct from the other aspects of the paschal mystery, is historically ascertainable. It was seen by human eyes, it happened in particular historical circumstances (e.g. under Pontius Pilate). This gives to his death and the life that led up to it, particular importance because it happens in the ways in which all our human actions and occurrences happen. Yet the resurrection and glorification of Christ spread a halo around the events of Jesus' life and death making them crucial to our understanding of God among us. So in the gospels Jesus' early disciples rewrite the whole of his life in the glow of the discovery of his resurrection.

The death of Jesus

To look at the death of Jesus we will ask the question: 'Why did Jesus die?'. We ask this question about the decisions, circumstances and attitudes which led to the process of law through which Jesus was put and which led to his execution. Human beings and human institutions gave origin to this process.

Jesus came to proclaim his Father's kingdom. All that Jesus did and said were about this kingdom: his words, his parables, his miracles. He called people to accept this kingdom and to act in response to his teaching, to follow him.

Initially it would seem there was a positive response to him and his preaching – even an enthusiastic response; but this response changed once it became

clear that he was not prepared to allow the expectations that others would seek to foist upon him to
distort his way of doing what the Father sent him to do.

Conflict is presented as a growing element in his
life, aroused by his words and actions and the response
of those who hear him. The gospels describe this as
coming from four different quarters:

from the people,

from his own disciples,

from leaders among the Jewish people,

from Pontius Pilate.

This conflict has a determining influence upon his
fate. The gospels present Jesus as being in conflict with
the people. They want to make him king; he will not
accept that. According to John 6:30ff, they come looking
for more bread the day after the feeding in the desert; he
will not give it to them but asks them to read what the
sign might mean. The people seek to foist upon Jesus
their own expectations about the messiah; he will not
even use this dangerous word about himself. This
foisting of expectations upon Jesus about what sort of
figure he should make of himself is in conflict with the
results of his own struggle to work out the way in which
he is to fulfil his mission. The narratives of the
temptations (Mt 4:1-11; Lk 4:1-13) capture this for us.
We see him tempted to the very things to which the
people in turn would tempt him. These he rejects
entrusting himself to the Father's way for him. The
kingdom he is proclaiming is not of the kind to which
the temptations urge him or to which the people are
urging him. He is not the kind of messiah that they are
urging him to be. This the people by and large find
unacceptable and so they do not find God's anointed in
Jesus. Here we have at work the lethargy, the deafness

to God's word, the blindness, the paralysis of human beings before what is for their good. The people want a 'bread and circuses' messiah which God will not give them. This manifests the lack of communion between God and human beings which we can discover in ourselves.

We see the same sort of dynamic at work between Jesus and his own disciples. They want him to be the sort of messiah they would like him to be. They seek to foist their own expectations onto him – wanting him to restore the kingdom to Israel (Acts 1:6); wanting the places on his right and left in his kingdom (Mt 20:20-23); not being content with this talk about his rejection and dying (Lk 18:31-34; 9:51-56). So we have the significant response of Jesus to Peter when Peter reprimands him for talking in this way: 'Get behind me, Satan, you think not as God thinks but as human beings think.' (Mt 16:21-23). This implied link between Satan and the way human beings think is an interesting link between what Jesus is tempted to in the temptation narratives and what he is tempted to by the people and by his own disciples.

In the gospel narratives we have many conflict stories between Jesus and various people in leadership positions in Israel (e.g. Mk 2:18-28; 3:1-6.22-30), Jesus does things which create difficulty for these people: he does not worry too much about the minute prescriptions into which the law has been cast; he eats with sinners and outcasts; he presents a kingdom whose arms stretch out to all. These sometimes small differences add up to his being seen as a threat to the law. For him the kingdom he proclaims comes out of Israel's tradition but it has a dominance in his mind and preaching which can place it above the law and its prescriptions. This is a source of conflict for those who see the law as dominant, as the only way to God. The fact that he eats with public sinners and publicans is a source of crisis for leaders in Israel as it makes him unclean and they themselves would become unclean if they ate with him.

Public sinners were seen as people who had stepped outside the covenant and so had made themselves unworthy of the covenant and of anyone taking it seriously. Such unclean people could not enter into Israel's worship. Jesus, by eating with them, asserted that the God he proclaims and the kingdom he proclaims do not exclude them. His act of eating with them is an invitation to companionship, to communion with him. This involves a conflict about who God is, what God is like and what God's attitude to the sinner is. We are approaching a delicate issue here, one which poses question marks to a way of understanding God which always has great potential for conflict. The same issues are at stake in the narrative of the adulterous woman (Jn 8:1-11); does God want the death of the sinner or does God want life for the sinner? Jesus presents here a re-orientation of the life of Israel in the light of the kingdom he proclaims.

On top of this, leaders in Israel are faced with Jesus as a potential source of disquiet among the people. Questions about who this man might be are in the air. He is talking kingdom-talk; he is performing miracles. Is he going to cause unrest among the people and bring down upon them yet again the heel of the Roman army? This produces an important political point of view concerning the disturbance he could cause among the people.

All of these points of conflict take on new poignancy when Jesus is brought before Pontius Pilate. Pilate is surrounded by forces pressing in on him – Jewish leaders, the crowd, his favour with Rome, and he has to choose to go along with these forces and allow Jesus to be condemned or to do justice to Jesus. The statement used by John: 'If you set him free you are no friend of Caesar's; anyone who makes himself king is defying Caesar' (19:12) has implications for Pilate's career. So when put on the spot Pilate chooses to feign that this is no business of his and allows Jesus to be put to death.

The death of Jesus is the result of human decisions, of human attitudes and of human circumstances. There were necessarily particular individual decisions involved in this about which we know little: those of Judas, of Pilate, of Jewish leaders for instance. But the whole situation leading to his death also involves things bigger than individual decisions; it involves human situations, states within which human beings lived their lives, attitudes aroused in or inherited by human beings which provided the context for individual decisions by particular people. It involves human institutions: the law, political forces, etc.

So there is involved what is often called the sinfulness of the world as a reality bigger than and precedent to the decisions of individuals. We can see two particular examples of this in Jesus' situation. There is the situation of Israel in Jesus' time: a nation under the occupying power of Rome. This brought out in Israel all the turmoil, unrest and violence that we see arise in a nation when another nation takes over and oppresses it. There were the guerilla forces in Israel seeking to be rid of the Roman power, there was the hatred of the Romans as the oppressors, there were the collaborators among the Jewish people working for the Romans and these, of course, were despised by the Jews. So Israel was in a volatile state and over the decades of Roman occupation there had arisen many claimants to messiahship causing unrest and uprisings among the people and further oppression from the Romans as they put the revolts down.

Jesus, without making any directly political claims, but by the very fact that he is present, speaking about a kingdom at such a time, means that he gets caught in this anxious and volatile situation and can become a prime object upon which the expectations of the people are focused. Their desire for liberation from the oppressor can seem to find all too easily a leader in Jesus who says and does extraordinary things among them. He was open to being interpreted politically and it is not too difficult to understand leaders among the Jews seeing in him just another troublemaker who would bring more suffering upon the people and produce no positive results.

There is a certain logic and social responsibility in the sentiment attributed to Caiaphas: 'You don't seem to have grasped the situation at all; you fail to see that it is better for one man to die for the people, than for the whole nation to be destroyed'. (Jn 11:49). John's Gospel sees this statement as prophetic (11:51); but it is also a statement of a politician in charge of people. We are not necessarily dealing with bad men but with men caught in a very human situation which they have in common with many other human beings before and after them.

Associated with this social situation is the fact that Pontius Pilate is caught in the web of 'jockeying for position' which was true for anyone in a high position in the Roman Empire at the time. Governorships were prestigious and profitable jobs, of which plenty of people were desirous, and which they would be prepared to seek at the cost of others' careers. The Jewish leaders had been to Rome over the decades before Pilate to rid themselves of unwanted rulers and this would have had to be in Pilate's mind. Here again we have a social situation in which a human being and his decisions are caught.

Jesus' attitude to his death

We need to change our perspective now to look at Jesus' death not from the point of view of those who would take his life from him but from his own point of view. What was his attitude to his approaching death in view of the increasing conflict arising around him and the increasing rejection he was experiencing?

Earlier on we mentioned those crucial narratives of the temptations of Jesus in the desert. These do not represent just one moment in the life of Jesus but they give expression to a dimension of the whole life of Jesus – his gradual discovery of the way he is to approach the mission given him by his Father. This rules his life. The narrative of Gethsemani is the completing of this discovery of his way. Again it is about a constant dimension of the life of Jesus and not just one moment of his life. Here he prays that the cup pass from him, that is, that his death pass from him; and yet if this is the continuation of the way he has come, then let it be. He is sent by the Father, not to die, but to proclaim the kingdom in word and deed. The rejection of this kingdom by human beings has led to conflict, rejection and death and so in that way fidelity to his mission from the Father will lead him into death. He hands himself over to death, in that same act handing himself over to the Father.

So his life is not taken from him against his will, and even though it is taken from him, he comes to see his death as a part of his mission from the Father and willingly hands himself over to his death and entrusts it into the Father's hands.

What killed Jesus?

Reflecting further on what was at work in the death of Jesus, we can identify in ourselves, in our relationships, and in our society, all of the elements which led to his death. We are not dealing with something which happened just then, but rather something which happened then and which continues to happen among us now, and which we can recognise as having happened throughout human history before and after Jesus. Those forces we saw earlier which brought about conflict between human beings and Jesus, and eventually brought about his rejection, are all present in every period of human history and have inflicted on others the sort of things which were inflicted on Jesus. These arose out of:

• the desire of the people to make the messiah in the image of their own expectations;
• the fact that Jewish leaders found him a threat;
• the reaction of an established religion to its being questioned;
• the ambition of Pilate;
• the ambiguity of Jesus' own disciples.

We can find all of these things and more in ourselves and, indeed, in our whole human race. Those people involved in the life of Jesus were not especially culpable; they were simply being human beings and were indeed symbolic of all of us: in a real sense they were ourselves involved in an encounter with him whom we have come to believe is himself the Word of God. This is crucial for our understanding of God present among us, and redeeming us in and through Jesus the Christ. So the death of Jesus is really the result of the situation in which humankind finds itself. This finds expression during Jesus' lifetime in the people, his disciples, Jewish leaders and Pontius Pilate; but it is a reality belonging to all of us that finds expression in them. We call this reality 'sin'.

Human sin brought about the death of Jesus: this power in our world which has been diminishing and distorting humanity through all of its history. It is part of each of us.

As Jesus becomes a part of that history which is ours, he will not allow the power of sin to penetrate his attitudes, his actions, his words, his relationships. He is sustained in this by his relationship to the Father.

In him, this sin finds a human being it cannot penetrate and the conflict which arises between him and the sinfulness of humanity will resolve this opposition once and for all. In that encounter, this fundamental human drama is played out.

Human sin brought Jesus to death. Yet how strange is the Father's resolution of this conflict – a resolution which does not take up power as we know it even to overcome this crushing sinfulness.

Human beings treat Jesus as 'the sinner', that is, his death is the death of a criminal. Criminals are those whom society's norms set aside as sinners. Jesus is executed. He is dealt with as one of those people who are not acceptable, not able to be integrated into human society because they are seen to threaten, diminish or destroy it. These people we imprison, exile or sometimes execute. They are what we mean by sinners in human societies. They are those who, like the public sinners in Israel, were seen no longer as part of the social contract by which a society survives. The public sinners in Israel no longer took part in the covenant since they were seen as having stepped outside of it and so were not able to enter into the exercise of that covenant in worship.... they were inimical to it. To mix with them made one unclean, that is, like them unable to enter into that excercise of the covenant which was Israel's worship. Some of these public sinners could be executed. The adulterous woman was one such; she could be executed by stoning.

Jesus is excluded not only from his society as criminal, but he is excluded also from the covenant. He is cast out of Israel, he has violated Israel's relationship with God. He is seen as an abomination to Israel. Anyone having anything to do with him is liable to share his fate – to be driven from the synagogue, excluded from the temple and so symbolically from the covenant relationship. So his disciples flee, go into hiding, live in fear of the Jews. They are traitors to Israel by their association with him.

Jesus becomes sin. He undergoes the treatment that human societies mete out to those they regard as beyond the acceptable. But in truth this is how we stand before God! This is what is revealed in the conflicts between Jesus and those who oppose him. In so far as he is God's Word to us, their opposition to him was an opposition to God even if they were blind and did not know what they were doing (see Lk 22:34). Here there is an exchange going on. Jesus becomes what we are: in his incarnation, he becomes flesh with us: in his death, he is dealt with in terms of the sin that is in us.

Further to this, a part of the struggle of Jesus that is presented to us in the gospels is his experience of abandonment. Out of his intimate experience of God as his own loving Father (Abba), he feels himself abandoned to his fate. Just as the sinner is cast aside by human society, is rejected and considered unworthy of human company, so Jesus has to struggle through this sense of being rejected, abandoned, set aside, cast out from the midst of humanity. All of this happens to him. But is it a matter of abandonment by the Father as well? His enemies do seem to triumph over him. God does not vindicate him but would seem to have left him to his fate. Yet is this not just the consequence of what the temptations meant, of what Gethsemani meant? Is this not also the moment to entrust himself into the strange hands of the Father?

All of this he takes into death. This human sinfulness that is cast upon him is stepping onto dangerous ground as it makes contact with Jesus because it will have to go through the process through which he is being led. Its apparent victory is a trap; it is caught and held in the action of his abandonment to the Father which is going to transform him and in him draw even this human sinfulness into his transformed life. This sin is going to meet, not a power like itself, but a love holding within it undreamt of power, power unlike anything human history had thrown up!

Everything that is ours he has taken to himself. As we will see, everything that is his he holds out to us to be ours!

The resurrection

The basic statement of faith in the resurrection is that the disciples of Jesus discovered him alive after his death; that he whom they knew during his earthly life in all its concreteness they now discover alive, still himself but very different. Now he is 'Lord'. All the resurrection narratives of the gospels, the Acts of the Apostles and the New Testament letters are clear on this. Indeed the evangelists have rewritten the whole gospel story of the earthly Jesus to proclaim this faith.

They assert that this risen Lord not only is risen but is the source of life from God for them. That contact with his person who has died and is now alive is the source of life and the overcoming of death and sin. These powers which had seemed to overwhelm Jesus in his death now are shown to be overcome by his resurrection. That sin which brought about the death of Jesus has been frustrated in its effects and the death in which it was operative has been transcended in that he lives.

The Father has taken the side of Jesus against these powers which hold such sway in our world. God has vindicated God's servant and shown Jesus to be the way, the truth and the life over against those who condemned him.

The Father has found the life of Jesus pleasing and has shown this in Jesus' glorification. The life of Jesus, his death and his resurrection now show us the way to the Father and what leads to communion with the Father.

The resurrection also summons up in the Jewish minds of Jesus' first followers, the coming of the end – that final action of God, a part of which will be the resurrection of the dead. Unexpectedly this happens only in Jesus but it sets up in them the expectation that he will return and that the resurrection of all will take place before very long.

The glorification of Jesus

We will draw out the further implications of the resurrection by talking about Jesus' return to his Father, or his ascension to God's right hand, or his glorification.

Jesus is not alive now with life as we know it. He has passed over to the Father and in that passing over he has entered into the life and glory of God. This has been manifested in his humanity. In his humanity and not just in his divinity he is glorified now and his risen human flesh is alive with the life of God and has become the source of that life for us. This is of course a highly relevant point for our purpose here which is to speak about the Eucharist where we have communication and communion with that life-giving Lord.

The humanity of Jesus – formed and fed out of our mother the earth and his mother, Mary of Nazareth – has now entered into the inner life of God, into the particular communion with the Father that belongs uniquely to the only begotten Son, who is the Father's beloved. As God has totally expressed God's self always in the beloved Son, we have the total expression of God's self in Jesus Christ, personally and totally divine and personally and totally human. As the Son has always given back to the Father a perfect responsive image of the Father, so now does the Father find that perfect, responsive image returning from the humanity of Jesus. This was all happening in the life of Jesus before his resurrection. It was this response that Jesus of Nazareth was struggling with in the temptations and at Gethsemani and it was this response that he gave.

This response of Jesus embodied in itself his being the perfect image of the Father, who gives us the most beloved Son that we might have life, that Son who is the supreme image of the love of God which is beyond our understanding.

Jesus' entry into the life of God does not entail his removal from our world and history; he is rather the first fruit that has been gathered in as a pledge of the whole harvest which is to come. Where he has gone, we are to follow. The presence of this glorified Lord to his community will always create a tension, therefore, and that tension is drawing us into his passover to the Father – a tension involving us in being called into his way as we see that lived out in his earthly life – a tension calling us to pass out of those attitudes which were operative in bringing about his death into the attitudes he showed in those same circumstances and conflicts.

Looking at all of this in another way: in Jesus' return to the Father, we have the reconciliation of human beings and God. We have a new communion established between God and humanity – more than we ever could have imagined that God would offer. This reconciliation is then presented to us so that what happened in Jesus might happen also in us, that it might, so to speak, expand into us, that we might enter into it as we receive it from God.

This new communion is wrought in the life, death, resurrection and glorification of Jesus. This is offered to us and having received it, it calls us to let it penetrate and possess us, drawing us into the Christian way of doing *now* in the circumstances of our life what Jesus did *then* in the circumstances of his life.

We have to discover in ourselves those forces which in the lifetime of Jesus impeded men and women from recognising and accepting him. These forces really do impede our communion with God and hold us in a state of alienation from God. So we go back constantly to the life of Jesus and focus it upon our lives as a means of discovering these negative forces in us and in society, and of discovering the movement of God's Word in us and in society. We do this so that we might allow the communion that Jesus has gained for us to get a deeper foothold in us and slowly to penetrate us to bring about in us the mind, the heart, the attitudes that were in him. This is a process of transformation which is lifelong; it is always new and yet in another sense, each of us has to set out on the same road yet again.

The sending of the Spirit

Pentecost is the gift of the Spirit poured out upon the disciples of Jesus. This sending of the Spirit is the birth of the Church.

The Spirit is the gift of God to us. The Spirit is the relationship between the Father and the Son. That relationship is the person of the Spirit. To receive that Spirit is to be caught up into that relationship.

The gift of the Spirit is the gift of the Risen Christ to us, he who is in communion with the Father as the Son, and who shares our humanity with us and draws our humanity up into God. The gift of the Spirit is that gift which sets off in us communion with God and passover into God with Christ.

It is by the gift of the Spirit that we can truly call God 'Abba' because that Spirit draws us into Christ's relationship with the Father, and is truly the Spirit of Christ. We now come before the Father with that Spirit creating in us Christ's intimate relationship with the Father, which was expressed in his earthly life in his calling God by the intimate name 'Abba' (Father).

It is the Spirit who makes us children of God in Christ who is the unique Son of God. By this Spirit we are interiorly adopted as children of God. Again we share in the relationship between Christ and the Father. There begins to emerge in our human lives, the life of Father, Son and Spirit, into which we have been taken.

There is yet another dimension to this. Since we have all received the same Spirit, we are drawn into communion with Christ and with each other. This finds expression in some beautiful images in the New Testament: that of body in St Paul (e.g. 1 Cor 12:12-30; Rom 12:4-5; Gal 3:28; Eph 4:4-6), the vine and the branches in chapter 15 of John's Gospel, the engrafting of a new branch on a tree (1 Cor 6:19); the idea of a spiritual temple made up of the many members of the Christian community (1 Cor 3:16; 2 Cor 6:16; Eph 2:20-22; Jn 2:21).

All of these images are pointing to an understanding of a union of life which later theology will express more fully and develop. When we look at these images, they all indicate a quite extraordinary reality: a union of life which is organic in its form of union. Like any image used to help us to see what we cannot see, we cannot pretend to exhaust what they lead us to but we can go some way along the road they indicate. Paul's image of the body is said by many exegetes to have an almost physical feel in the way he uses it. He speaks of the followers of Jesus as being 'sosomos' (embodied) with him (Rom 6:1-11) of being 'in Christ' (Rom 6:1-11; Gal 2:20; Phil 1:21); of being like the organs of a body all living the same life and functioning as a unity (1 Cor 12). The human body is an image of this union. The image used in John 15 has the same sense of common life and organic unity. Jesus is the vine; we are the branches of the vine. All live the life of the same tree – the sap runs through them giving life. So similarly, the image of engrafting: the engrafted branch of the tree takes in the sap of the tree and begins to live as a native branch of the tree.These images are opening up for us what it means to be drawn into communion with Jesus Christ by the gift of his Spirit and so to be drawn into communion with the Father. This is the gift we receive in receiving the gift of the Spirit of God.

Unity will be always crucial to this. The narrative of Pentecost is written by Luke with one eye on the narrative of the Tower of Babel. The latter is the story of humankind's dispersion symbolised in the division of languages which prevents solidarity and harmony, which creates the division and the scattering of humanity. At Pentecost, all the peoples hear the word about Jesus in their own languages which no longer impede their unity. By the gift of the Spirit of God, all these peoples can find unity in Christ.

In this gift of the Spirit, the Church came to birth. The disciples of Jesus are drawn into his passover. As the Church, we are in a state of passover from being human as we know that now, to being human as we will know that in the risen Lord. He draws us into his life and relationship with the Father. Essentially this is something happening, not something which has happened. We are his body in tension with him. There is present in us both humanity as it manifested itself in those in opposition to Jesus, and humanity in a communion with Jesus as we are being drawn into the new and true humanity as manifested in him.

In brief, all that is in humanity is in the Church, and all that is in Christ is in the Church, which is the passover into Christ as he seeks to bring about in us what came about in him. We have died with Christ in our baptism into communion with him and we have been raised to new life.

By the fact that Christ takes possession of us as his own, as his body, we give him 'body' in our world. This does not limit or contain his presence much less exhaust it. Rather, it gives his presence a 'body'.

The Church – the community of believers – in all its diversity and complexity is the end-product of the paschal mystery. The death and resurrection of Jesus culminates in a communion of life established between the dead and risen Lord and the community of his disciples, who are characterised by being caught up into his passover.

When this group comes together to celebrate the Eucharist, it is this passover which they celebrate as the very source of their identity, as the very source of the transformation Christ is inviting them into as a gift intended for the whole of the human race.

The Church is, therefore, of its very nature, an eschatological reality. When we speak of the Church in this sense, we are speaking always of what is and what is not yet. It is, of its nature, something becoming. It cannot be itself until Christ comes again! It cannot be understood or spoken of save as a history, as something coming about. So the mystery of the Church is not something substantive hidden somewhere within or behind or beyond the concrete historical reality of the world.

It is the manifestation of the working of God in Christ by means of the Spirit in human history. It is this working of God embodying itself in an historically actual group of people. It is the Father drawing them into communion in Christ in the unity of the Holy Spirit. This communion is coming-to-be. It will be so until Christ comes again. The Church is, of its very nature, this eschatological tension between what is, and what is coming to be.

Having looked at the paschal mystery in some detail we will now move on to examine the meaning of the basic word associated with the Eucharist in the New Testament and in much of the tradition: memory. All the Eucharistic Prayers tell us that we do what we do in the the Eucharist in memory of Christ's death and resurrection. The human reality opened by this word provides the link between the Eucharist and the death and resurrection of Christ.

Reflection

1. What link do you see between those things which brought about the death of Jesus and the forces at work in your own daily life?

2. How do you understand the sinfulness present in the Church in the light of the life, death and resurrection of Jesus?

3. Have you developed a clearer meaning of participating in the Eucharist in the light of this chapter?

2 | *Memorial*

'Do this in memory of me.' These words given us in the Lukan and Pauline institution narratives and, we can say, presumed in the Marcan and Matthean forms[1] oblige us to take up the notion of memorial if we wish to develop any understanding of the meaning of the action we are performing in the Eucharist.

Memorial in Israel

There is an understanding of memorial already at work in Israel which flows into New Testament times and is at work in the New Testament understanding of the Eucharist. In the Old Testament there is a significant use of words like 'remember', 'memory' and 'memorial' which make these words imply not just an inner psychological activity but an activity having dynamic effect beyond the remembering person. There was not in the Old Testament the sort of implied separation of thought and action which we can presume. Human action was seen as a single dynamic activity involving what we would tend to separate out as thought and action. This was not unique to Israel, but true for ancient peoples in general. It is true in our spontaneous action.

In our more systematic reflection we can speak about thought or remembering as an activity occurring purely within the inner workings of the human mind. We can see memory as merely a recalling going on within us. Memory can be spoken about also as a storage faculty of the mind wherein we retain images or experiences of the past. Our actual use of the word, however, often goes beyond such conceptions. A mother can say to her child 'remember what happened last time you did that'. She is not urging a purely reflective activity in the child but that the child's remembering produce action, flow through into the action of not doing what it was proposing to do.

We frequently use the word in this way in our ordinary speech. This usage comes close to the biblical use of this word. It is used to produce or prevent action. 'To remember' is to move into action. When God is asked to remember someone God is asked to act in accord with past contact with that person. So when God is asked to remember the covenant, God is being asked to act towards the people in accord with the covenant God made with them at Sinai, to let that flow into effect now. When God is asked to remember Abraham, or David, or Moses, God is being asked 'to credit to their account' the fidelity which they showed to God or to credit that fidelity to the people's account now.[2]

When Israel is called to remember, it is being called to act likewise in accord with the covenant commitment, to be faithful to the keeping of the law which God gave them on Sinai. Remembering is a form of contact with the past but a past which is seen as having its repercussions and implications in the present, even as flowing into the present.

In *Memory and Tradition in Israel*, Brevard Childs links the development of 'memory' in Israel's prayer and thought to the development of their tradition.[3] This arises through their developing understanding of how they have contact in the present with the founding events of their nation and with the covenant which ensued from those events. So the Deuteronomist writers suggest that Israel's obedience to the law given by God in the present is the way in which they now encounter the God their ancestors encountered on Sinai in the past. This gift of the law was a gift of God's Word by obedience to which Israel comes to know the God of the exodus as the giver of freedom; they know God in the present as the law releases them from slavery to false idols. When one obeys the law, remembering the events of the exodus and of Sinai, one obeys the Law in memory of these events: 'Remember what God did in the exodus and keep God's law!' In this way one discovers that same liberating God.

Similarly the psalmists in the psalms of lamentation are calling out to God for deliverance. But they do this by remembering the events by which God has delivered the people in the past. The psalmists, in their present situation, call out to God to deliver them as God delivered the people in the past. This remembering is the source of the turnabout in their prayer to confidence and trust in the God who continues to deliver the people.

In these prayers, as part of the religious life of Israel, the present actuality of the initial events is being experienced in faith as they are remembered. They are seen not as inert or distant but as something to be called upon in the present. The God who did these things in the past is being discovered involved in the same sort of activities in the present. God is doing now in different circumstances, what God did then.

Israel's worship is permeated entirely by memorial. Whenever Israel comes before God in worship, it is to call to God's mind the covenant God has made with them and to which God has promised fidelity. They come before God to keep going the flow of memory between God and themselves – to keep receiving the loving mercy which was the motivation for the covenant God made with them. But this remembering is mutual. They engage in worship to remember God and God's covenant and also to remember their commitment to God's law in order that they may continue to receive the covenant and to be God's faithful, covenanted people.[4] All the signs of their worship embodied this: the clothing of the priests; the arrangement of the temple; the psalms which made up their prayer. These were all memorials whose purpose was to remind God of the covenant with Israel and to remind Israel of its covenant with God.

In this flow of memory the covenant was maintained. In all of this, a relationship between past and present was presupposed, worked out of, and developed.

Memory: further reflection

In developing our understanding of memory we need to take up further the point made above about the relationship between the past and the present. Events in history occur at a specific time and place and they are unrepeatable. They belong to their own moment in history and no other. Yet events in history are dynamic: they do not happen and then cease but rather they happen and bring about something which continues. They introduce a modification or a re-shaping, however slight, of what was there before them. They do occur indeed at a fixed time and in a fixed place but they are not exhausted wholly by that time and place but transcend it by what they introduce into the ongoing flow of history or life.

This is true for something as ordinary (and extraordinary) as each of our own births. We are the result of the union of our parents – we come from that event not just physically but psychologically and socially. Their conceiving us and then giving us birth happened at a particular time and in a particular place. This is a beginning but it is not an end. It gives origin to a new human person who will effect the world in which he or she lives; this very presence will modify and reshape the world in all sorts of small (and perhaps large) ways. This is true equally of social and political events: a new country is settled, a new political party with new policies is voted into power, an economic downturn creates a new level of poverty in a society. All of these are events or series of events which have ongoing presence in the line of human history of which they are a part. So the exodus occurred in Israel and brought about a new form of Israel's relationship with God. They were a people who saw themselves as shaped by that event, even taking their identity from that event, which created a new sense of themselves and of what their history was about.

Memory is not just something we learn about from the bible. What we see at work in the scriptures is something which is an inherent dimension of our human life, something which has to be there if we are to be human beings. Memory is about the fact that we are historical beings, whose identities are shaped by the very flow of our lives. This is true of us both as individuals and as social groups.

What we are describing here are originating events, that is, events which give origin to something which continues. Memorial is about the present effects of a past event, still operative among us. These events we celebrate in memorial celebrations. Our birthday celebrations are memorials: we celebrate this person through their origin, their birth; we celebrate the fact that that event has given origin to the person whom we are honouring by this celebration. Any anniversary celebration is the same. It celebrates what is now by celebrating what gave it origin, be this a wedding anniversary, the anniversary of a death or the anniversary of the founding of a nation. Reaching back in memory is something we do without even thinking about it. These originating events continue to shape the present: our personalities, national movements, ongoing realities like the Church.

Let me take some examples which will show how radically we are ourselves 'memorials'. If a people get to a point in their lives where they are blocked in their personal development, a counsellor will invite them to go back in memory to some point in their lives where there is a sort of psychological knot that is causing the present difficulty. Something has happened in their life (history, memory) which disables them in the present from getting on with their lives in a happy, healthy and fruitful manner. They will live out of that difficulty until they go back to it and untie the knot cutting off their psychological blood supply. Here memorial is at work. They will probably have some sort of 'memorial celebration' in the present to get at this past: some method of giving it present form so as to deal with it.

An example in social-political life is given to us in any of our present world trouble spots. If we take the troubles in Northern Ireland as a well-known example, what we have happening there is a society which was set up along discriminatory lines with the power arranged to be always in the hands of one section of the community. This society and the hatred that reigns in it are the result of events which happened back in the seventeenth century. One of these events which we will use for the purposes of our argument was the Battle of the Boyne in which William of Orange, the then King of England, defeated James II who was seeking to gain power in Ireland and then in England. William was the Protestant, James the Catholic. Out of this defeat the Protestant ascendency was set up in Ireland and continues now in some form in the six counties which make up the British province of Northern Ireland. On 12 July every year this victory of William over James at the Battle of the Boyne is celebrated. It gains heartfelt response from those Protestants who identify strongly with the whole establishment of the Protestant ascendancy.

There was a line of history established by the events back in the seventeenth century. Of those events, the present Northern Ireland society and its troubles are the present effects. The past event still bears its fruits in our time. On 12 July each year, when these original events are held up before people in banners, songs, marches and speeches, the events are imbibed again and give the people present a sense of identity and solidarity in the same ascendency that was set up in the originating events. The present celebrations continue to enforce the convictions and the fears along with the violence which result from them. The society of Northern Ireland continues to live out of, and to live out, these events which gave origin to it.

The same may be said of difficulties between the peoples of Croatia, Serbia and Bosnia-Herzogovina, of troubles between Moslems and Hindus in India, of difficulties between French-speaking and English-speaking Canadians, of troubles between Basques and Spaniards. Closer to home, we have our current tensions between Aboriginal and non-Aboriginal Australians which arise out of events in the past which have dispossessed and marginalised Aborigines. All of these social-political situations are a living out of historical events which have so marked the histories of these peoples and their relationships that it becomes a pulse according to which they live. In all of this, the human reality we name 'memorial' is at work.

I have tended to take examples of troubled situations because they are so clear. But the same process is at work in the good happenings in our lives. We know that we can trust people because in the past they have shown themselves trustworthy. This memorial structure of human life penetrates everything, is so much part of us that we can fail to notice its presence. So significant events introduce a new modification into human reality, personally or socially, and that continues on as a dynamic part of that reality.

We need to note also that this is not just a matter of one event. Other events occur which will be seen in line with the original event or maybe even open up further some part of the meaning of that original event which had not yet been noticed.

We are not dealing with a passive process. In each generation, new events occur, new insights are gained, new perspectives are taken up within the line of development originating in the past events. Reinterpretation keeps occurring within this tradition of memory, the remembered event can take on new 'hues' from the later experience of the people who find continuing history confirming, or deepening, what has been lived out and lived out of. The memory of the exodus in Israel a is typical example of this. The original event became more and more determinative of the people's history as other events occurred which showed them the activity of the God of the exodus. There was a certain telescoping of events. They were living in a new sense of history because of the exodus and this sense of history led them to keep rediscovering the pattern of the exodus in other events.

The dynamic of memory does not involve only past and present but it involves also the future, that is, it sets up in us an approach to our life and history, establishing in us expectations and a way of seeing the world within which we enter into our future. This is true for all the examples given above. We are projected into our future on the basis of our formation in the past.

There are two levels involved in memorial: there is the actual modification of reality brought about by the event, and there is our consciousness of this or our remembering of it. An event occurs and changes the previous situation e.g. the birth of a child, the settling of a new nation such as Australia or the United States of America, the arrival of waves of new migrants in a country. But these events have to be remembered for us to allow them to alter our consciousness, or for them to become truly part of an individual's identity. So, for instance, parents have to remember that they have a new child, that is, they have to act as if they have a new child, the change has to enter their consciousness or the life of their child will go awry. When a country accepts a new flow of migration, the make-up of its population changes but this may not be recognised explicitly. It can attempt to go on as if these new people were having no effect on the shaping of the national identity. This event has to be remembered, lived out and lived out of, so that the national consciousness and the actual people who make up the nation achieve some sort of integration.

In this remembering we come to self-possession, we grasp who we are. Without this remembering, we cannot come to self-possession as individuals or as social groups. Since our memory is constitutive of our identity, to leave someone out of our individual memory (e.g. to reject a parent) or to leave groups of people in a nation out of the common memory or identity is to ignore something which is constitutive of that identity. It is also to refuse self-possession: in the case of the individual, it is to create marginalised areas of our own personalities which will prove troublesome to our continuing life; in the case of the social group, it is to create marginalised groups in society which will stir up trouble for the accepted common identity of the group or even become violent towards the established identity (memory) of the group. This is evidenced clearly in the movement for civil rights by black people in the United States of America; it is evident in the women's movement all over the world. The common memory is always lacking in inclusiveness with regard to some people or some dimension of its reality. When this comes to our notice we have to seek to recover that part of our memory if we are to continue to move towards self-possession. We must remember who we are.

Our memory is ourselves as historical beings. Our identity is in our memory – it constitutes us in our sense of self individually and communally. When people lose their memory, they lose their identity; we lose them and they lose their place in human community. We can no longer perceive them in their own identity as once we did. They are lost to us.

To remember is to take possession of all that has gone into our making. It brings us into contact with those people and those events and relates us to them in such a way that they come to be in us and bear their fruit in us. In this we become ourselves. Our personal identity and the identity of social groups are rooted deeply in solidarity with others and with our world.

Memory: symbol

This same memory is at work in our use of symbols. Let us take, for example, a photograph. We can recognise a person in a photograph only if that person has a place in our memory. So memory and recognition are linked. It is only if we have seen this person or thing before and remember them that we can recognise and name them. We have what we might call an internal image within us which enables us to recognise the external image presented to us in the photograph. A photograph that moves us deeply (e.g. of a person dear to us who has died) can do so only because it has the capacity to summon up this internal image within us and identify that image with itself. In this it enables us to come into contact with that internal image. A national anthem does the same thing within the social group of a nation: the anthem expresses the nation's identity; it gives a means by which that identity can come to expression. Any sort of memorial celebration falls back upon the same dynamic. This is what symbolism is all about and it functions on the basis of memory. This will be important for us when we come to the explicit consideration of the Eucharist.

It is useful to note that memory acts spontaneously in our world and our history as a whole, before there is any separating out of the subjective and objective dimensions of our world. Speaking of the subjective and objective dimensions of our whole existent world as if they were separated sections of it, has been a cause of misconceptions in eucharistic theology, as in other areas of thought. This is a useful distinction but it is not a separation of a world into two different spheres.

To sum up: in remembering we call forth an image or set of images which has been charged with significance by the past where it has been associated with specific events. It acts now to bring us into contact with that event so as to see ourselves as being in some way rooted in it, as deriving some dimension of our continuing existence from it. It is constitutive of us in the present.

Theology of memorial

In the light of what we have drawn out about memorial, let us look again at memorial in Israel. There is a toughness to the use of memorial in the scriptures because God is involved. The word that goes forth from God's mouth will not be revoked, it bears God's own solidity or fidelity within it. The people keep reminding God of the firmness of God's commitment to them in the covenant so that God will continue to act in their regard in accord with that same fidelity.

God's great act of delivering the people from Egypt is the sign of this fidelity upon which all of Israel's relationship with God falls back. In the exodus, God is revealed as the saviour of the people and they kept expecting that God would be just what those acts showed God to be – saviour. God was indeed the God of the exodus! And they would implore God to do again in our days what was done in those great days (e.g. Hab 3:2-4; Pss 63:7; 77:4.7).

In an article on 'The Church and Pentecost', Yves Congar puts very clearly the role of these great events. He says that they were the decisive acts or moments selected by God to reshape forever an existing relation between God and human beings. In celebrating a memorial of these events Israel puts itself in the current of God's gift – so God works to effect in time what was initiated in the event. 'His acts – like himself – were, are and are to come'.[5] Israel lives in memorial of these events and in every act of its worship makes memorial of them.

Israel enters into its continuing history in memory of this event of the exodus, that is, expecting to find in that history the God of the exodus; expecting constantly that in some form the exodus would be renewed. The exodus was the event of God's self-revelation and Israel carries the exodus into its history to create an interaction between the exodus event and every other time or stage of its history. In so doing, Israel discovers the God of the exodus at work in those other times. So it is 'in memory of the exodus' that Israel struggles to interpret everything; it is 'in memory of the exodus' that it seeks to receive every other event, every other stage of its history: it is 'in memory of the exodus' that it keeps rediscovering the life-giving God who is with it as it lives out its history.

The exile in Babylon is a good example of this. In this moment of their history, God seems to have deserted the Jews. All of the things they had received as a result of the exodus had been taken from them, even the land itself had been lost. They were, therefore, 'tempted to hang up their harps by the waters of Babylon', to wonder whether they could 'sing the songs of Zion in this foreign land'. That is, they wondered if the covenant was at an end and their worship pointless. In this desperate situation, the prophets urge them to go back to the exodus, to bring to bear on their present plight the act of God delivering them from slavery in Egypt. In this they find their new beginning, and begin to call Babylon, Egypt; they see their return to the land of Israel as a journey through a desert like the one of old, as they enter into a new stage of their history and their relationship with God in the covenant.

We need to notice that this is not a simplistic process of repetition of the exodus: it is a discernment of the God of the exodus acting anew in fidelity to God's self-revelation in the exodus. It also requires that the people work this out. There is a struggle involved and a genuine discernment in the present. In all of this, they learn about God who is working among them anew. Their struggle to recognise God at work results in a new perception of God.

The memorial of Jesus

'Do this in memory of me.' Christians live in memory of Jesus Christ – of his life, death and resurrection. It is this event which they take with them into each new event and each new stage of their history.

The death and resurrection of Jesus, as we saw in the previous chapter, results in a new relationship between God and human beings 'in Christ'. This is the sense behind Paul's statement that we are baptised into Christ (Rom 6:3; Gal 3:27), that we are plunged into this new reality of relationship with God in Jesus who is the anointed one of God. The event of his death and resurrection originates this continuing relationship entered into through Baptism. It is this relationship with Jesus Christ which gives us our specific identity as the community of believers, the Church. It is 'in the memory of Jesus' that we discover who we are and are enabled to live in the way of Jesus.

In the Eucharist, to rephrase the earlier quotation from Congar, we put ourselves in the current of God's gift, God's working to effect in time what God initiated on that particular day.

This means that we enter into each new stage of our lives, each new stage of human history, bearing with us the memory of the death and resurrection of Jesus as our way of discovering at work the God who raised Jesus from death, and brought him into his glory. It is in memory of the death and resurrection of Jesus that in each situation of our history we seek to discern God's leading us and all humanity into the future that all of humankind will share, a communion with God in the kingdom which we, the disciples of Jesus, have accepted in the name of all.

The Eucharist has to do not just with those who are now disciples of Jesus but with all of humankind whose future is assured in the raising of Jesus out of death into communion with the Father. We are called to live in his memory in order that the mystery of the coming of God's kingdom for which Jesus died, might continue in all times and in all places until he comes again.

As we celebrate the Eucharist in his memory we tap into God's working 'to effect in time' what God brought about in the death and resurrection of Jesus. We bring to the Eucharist everything that is present in our human race, all the goodness and potential, all the sinfulness and blindness that we saw at work in Jesus' life. This is all in us. We are our world; we should not be surprised that whatever is in humanity of good or ill can be found abundantly in the Church. It is only in this way that we can fulfil our mission to be those human beings in whom our world, as it is, meets explicitly its redeeming Lord, Jesus, the holy one of God. All that brought him to his death and continues on its destructive way in our world is in us. And in us meets him who has been raised from the death brought upon him by this human destructiveness. In the community of faith the Father's continuing activity is revealed. The Father continues to do what was done in the death and resurrection of the Son – to overcome the power of sin and death in our world. The Father does this by drawing us into communion with the Son by the power of the Spirit who is poured out upon us. Thus the Father continues to effect in time what was brought about on the day of Jesus' resurrection.

As Jesus in his humanity passed over into life with the Father, so are we caught up into such a communion with Jesus by the Spirit of Pentecost that we are tensed into passover from humanity as it is among us now, to humanity as it is in Jesus. The Eucharist is the continuation of Pentecost – the gift of the Spirit who unites us to Jesus and to each other in a communion of life. It is noticeable that we never make memorial of Pentecost in the anamnesis of the Eucharist because the Eucharist is the gift of the Spirit of the risen Lord catching us up into communion with that same risen Lord. We make memorial of that which brings that about: the death, resurrection and glorification of Jesus.

In the Eucharist, we come before the Father in that action which Jesus gave us to do in his memory, that action in which he gave himself over to the Father. We are invited to join him in that handing over to the Father in order that the Father 'might see and love in us what you (Father) see and love in Christ'[6] in order that the work of redemption might be embodied in us within our world.

In this structured action of a ritual meal we are given the means to enter into communication and communion with Christ in word and action. This ritual meal feeds into us the communion between ourselves and Christ enabling us to be caught up into his passover. It is only by our communion with him that this is possible. It is in a meal with all its rich symbolism of human and divine communion that our communion with Jesus is expressed and established. We will look into this further as we proceed.

As we enter into this meal of Eucharist, we bring all the unfinished business of our lives and of human history into communion with Jesus Christ in whom we will find fulfilment. A passing over into him is established in that communion.

So in this communion between Jesus and his disciples 'in memory' of his death and resurrection, the Father is bringing about in us what the Father brought about in Jesus. As Jesus handed himself over to the Father, so is the Father bringing about in us this attitude of handing ourselves over to God in all the circumstances of our lives and history.

Just as the Father moved towards Jesus to raise him from the power of death and sin in response to Jesus' abandonment, so the Father moves towards us in the Eucharist, giving us new life that death cannot overcome. The Father credits to us what occurred in the death of the Son as we do this action in memory of

Jesus' death. We are being given new life in our communion with Jesus Christ, a life which death cannot overcome. The Father sees in the face of the Church, the face of the beloved Son as the Church engages in this action in memory of that Son.

This involves the two-directional remembering that we spoke of in regard to the Old Testament. We celebrate the Eucharist as the memorial of Christ, moving towards the Father in communion with Christ. The Father responds to us as to Christ since we come before the Father in Christ's memorial. In the Third Eucharistic Prayer we ask the Father to look upon our offering and see Christ, the 'victim whose death has reconciled us to himself'. The flow of memory is the continuing of our covenant relationship to God in Christ.

All of this extraordinary communion of life is expressed in the doxology of the Roman Eucharistic Prayers : 'Through him, with him, in him, in the unity of the Holy Spirit, all glory and honour is yours, Almighty Father, forever and ever'. This communion is that which we saw the New Testament writers struggling to express in their vivid images 'body', 'vine and branches', 'engrafting'.

Memorial celebration

What we do in memory of Jesus is a particular action – a ritual meal – which takes its meaning out of its place in human culture and society, out of its use in the religion of the Old Testament and out of the Christian history of its use. This action is for the Christian community what the birthday celebration is as a memorial celebration, and what the 12 July celebration

on the streets of Northern Ireland is for the main-
tenance of a particular state of that society. We are
involved in the same human dynamic.

Our sacraments are human signs or symbols which
are made different by the fact that they are signs of
something new – the paschal mystery of Jesus. St
Thomas makes this clear in his treatment of sacraments
in the *Summa Theologiae* where he defines sacraments as
'sacrae rei signa sanctificantis homines' that is, 'signs of a
sacred reality which sanctifies human beings'[7]. The
sanctifying is attributed to the sacred reality of which
the sacraments are signs and not to the signs as such
which are left in the normal 'genus' of sign rather than
being put into the special category of *'signum efficax'*
(efficacious sign).[8]

Now symbols work not as isolated realities but in
relationship to the human group which uses them.
Their meaning is not in themselves but in the society or
culture within which they function as symbols. So the
symbols used on 12 July (banners, songs, speeches,
marches, etc) draw something out from Northern
Ireland society; as does the playing of the football
game for the supporters; as does the flag and anthem
for a nation. The symbols have their significance in
something beyond themselves but to which they
belong intrinsically. They function in such a way that
they can draw out the inner identity of the group to
which they relate as symbols.

So in singing a national anthem, people find
themselves experiencing their 'nationality'; this inner
identity finds a way to express itself in and through
something else – the anthem which is a symbol
outside of themselves but which has power within
them. This could not happen if those people did not

belong to that nationality. This is how the eucharistic action works.

If I might take up again the example of the photograph I used earlier. The photograph has significance for us in so far as it has the capacity to capture in itself the interior image of the person. It acts as a symbol which can draw from within us the interior image of the person and enable us to experience that person memorially. It is all about memory. Memorial and symbol are two different ways of looking at the same thing – the latter emphasises the present occurrence of symbolic presence, the former looks at what enables that to occur: the past built into us.

When we celebrate the Eucharist, this action has the capacity to enable us to enter into communication with what makes us Church – communion with Christ.

Eucharist is the high point of our initiation into the Church, that is, it is the action by which the Church expresses its own identity. As individuals, we are initiated into the Church – either by our upbringing in the course of which the Church's tradition can become our own inner conviction, or by a process of conversion which leads us to identify with the Church. By our initiation, we take on belonging to the Church as part of our identity. Our initiation processes aim for (and achieve) a sense of identity rather than simply knowledge or individual holiness. The high point of this is Eucharist. This is where the Church sees itself as most itself.

So what the Eucharist does is not portrayed well in an image such as that of Jesus coming down from heaven on to the altar because it presumes a Christ absent from his Church. Rather, the Eucharist is our means of recognising Christ present in his Church: the first disciples recognised him and we recognise him in the breaking of the bread! This recognition is rooted in memory! It is the Christ who continues present among us who is recognised present when the community gathers to do the actions he did on the night before he died. Eucharist is not just about Christ's presence but about Christ's presence in his Church, the community of believers. This recognition is an act of the Church, and of the individual as one who has been initiated into the Church.

In the Eucharist the Church's own inner identity is put out before us. This is the meaning of Augustine's often quoted phrase: 'It is your own mystery.'[9] What happens in the Eucharist is not something strange to us or outside of ourselves but the encountering of our own deepest identity as the Church, the identity of which is its being a communion with and in Christ.

There is a very strong sense of Eucharist among the Fathers of the Church which is expressed in the phrase: *'Ecclesia facit Eucharistiam et Eucharistia facit Ecclesiam'*[10] – the Church celebrates (makes) the Eucharist and the Eucharist establishes (makes) the Church. The Church which gathers to do what Jesus did, recognises Christ's presence in its midst and enters into his action before the Father with him. But this eucharistic action makes the Church and establishes it in its very identity. The Eucharist is 'the real, reciprocal presence' of Christ and his Church.[11] This occurs in the first instance in the common action of Christ and his Church in the Eucharist which is first and foremost an action of the Church in Christ, and of Christ in his Church.

It is also important to refer again to a point made above. This eucharistic action does not presume the absence of Christ who becomes present only in the course of the Eucharist, but the presence of Christ in his Church which is recognised eucharistically and is given this further eucharistic form in bread and wine in order that we can enter into further communion with him.

This approach fits in with the traditional structure of the sacraments as described by St Thomas Aquinas. He speaks of the *sacramentum tantum* (the sacrament or sign only), the *sacramentum et res* (the sign which is also a reality) and the *res tantum* (the ultimate reality of the sacrament).[12] The Eucharistic liturgy (or, in our examples, the photograph or the singing of the national anthem) is the sign or sacrament only; the recognition in faith of Christ's presence (the interior image of the person or the recognition of our national identity) is the reality which is itself in turn a sign; and the unity of the Church in Christ (or our union with the person photographed or the reinforcement of our national identity) is the ultimate reality of the symbolic process.

This is an important point because we have come out of a period of the Church's history where we have tended to see the presence of Christ in the bread and wine of the Eucharist as the culminating point of the Eucharist. This results to a large extent from the experience of centuries of generations of Christians receiving communion very infrequently. Communion was not a part of their normal experience of the Mass. Venerating Christ's presence was a much more dominant factor in their lives than entering into communion with him present in the Eucharist. This mentality inevitably became dominant. However the Eucharist was given us originally that we might enter into communion with Christ, which communion with him constitutes us his Church. St Thomas' above distinction makes this clear but it has not been a strong part of Catholic consciousness for many centuries. The full course of the Eucharist's action is that we take to ourselves in the bread and wine of the Eucharist, the entire mystery unfolded in the Eucharist's course. Church 'makes' Eucharist, Eucharist 'makes' Church.

Thomas Aquinas also speaks of the Eucharist as *'signum commemorativum'*, *'signum demonstrativum'*, *'signum prognosticum'* (a sign rooted in the past, which actually presents something to us in the present and which anticipates the future.[13] The Eucharist is grounded in the past events of Christ's passion or passover. It presents to us now the fruits of that passover in our participation in Christ and it gives us now a foretaste of that future glory towards which we are tensed by our communion with and in Christ. All of this belongs to the memorial nature of the Eucharist:

- it is founded in the past event of Christ's death and resurrection;
- it gives us now participation in the fruits of that paschal mystery by means of the Spirit who creates a communion between Jesus and us and therefore in Jesus with the Father;
- it sets us up to expect that the Father will continue to do what was done in the death and resurrection of Jesus as we move into the future.

We live out of, and we live out, the event of Jesus' death in all that it means. These two phrases 'live out of' and 'live out' express very well what it means to be the memorial of something. We 'live out of' and 'live out' his death or his death and resurrection are phrases which capture well what has been said about memorial. It is about both our identity and our approach to life and history which involves the ethical dimension of life.

This implies constant interaction between ourselves and the life and death of Jesus. It implies that we are seeking always in our lives the God who does now what was done in Jesus, that we live out our lives in the way of Jesus in order to be able to discover this same God at work. So it is that nothing ever can replace the narratives of the life of Jesus for us since they are not a matter of information, history or catechesis. Rather, we live in interaction with them in order to find now what God was doing then, and it is out of this process that the living Word of God emerges for us now. It is the movements in our lives, the decisions we are called to make which stand out for us when we place the grid of the scriptual narratives over our own lives and they lock into place as moments of encounter with God in Christ in our own situation.

Our use of the scriptures is also a matter of memorial. We listen to the word also in memory of him. Word and Eucharist belong together.

The word of the scriptures which we proclaim invites us now into an encounter with Christ such as his first disciples had during his lifetime. His word seeks to lead us on the journey on which they were led into communion with him. This found supreme expression in their doing what he did on the night before he died, the Lord's Supper. The gospel narratives have been written presuming this later encounter of the first Christian communities with the risen Lord in line with the encounter of the disciples during Jesus' earthly life. As documents, the gospels presume a structure based on 'what happened then – happens now' and they often telescope into one the two stages of Christian history – the encounter of the first disciples with the Lord on earth and the encounter of the later disciples with the risen Lord.

Living out his resurrection out of death

There are consequences to our celebration of the Eucharist which arise out of our relationship to the event or events of Jesus' death and resurrection. Celebrating his memory means that our life as a Christian community and as Christian individuals is given its direction by this event. We are not just living out of, and living out, his resurrection and leaving behind us his death and what leads to it because they have been overcome in his resurrection. The word 'passover' and the passover imagery of the New Testament and of the liturgy is significant: we celebrate his passover through death into risen life, or to the Father. There is indeed a focus upon his death. It is the immediate focus both of the words of Jesus over the bread and cup in the institution narratives and of Paul's presentation of the Eucharist in chapter eleven of his first letter to the Corinthians as a proclamation of his death. His death and what leads up to it are recognisable to us as human events, the resurrection we believe in faith.

The Christian mystery and the Eucharist which expresses it, is a mystery of Jesus' passover. The Eucharist is a mystery of our participation in that passover. Participation in the Eucharist, therefore, involves us in the memorial of the circumstances within which Jesus' death occurred and what is revealed about humanity in those circumstances as we saw them in the chapter on paschal mystery. It involves the memorial of the whole life of Jesus as his gradually-discovered way to be the

Father's servant. It involves Jesus' death as a decision taken about him by others, and it involves his death as his own free choice, as an act of love and worship. Our participation in his passover involves us in the memorial of his resurrection, his glorification and his being made source of the Spirit. It is the event *out of* which we live and which we live *out*, and with which we must live in interaction so as to live the Christian life in our world.

The death of Jesus is particularly important as are the events leading up to it because they are events which are historically ascertainable and whose like are still happening identifiably among us.

When we eat this bread and drink this cup we proclaim his death until he comes; that is, we proclaim his death as our way ahead, as our source of life and our way to God until he comes and manifests himself again.[14] We trust in his death, we believe it has borne fruit for all humankind. Through all of human history we celebrate this death which opens up the future, as the source of life and yet it was the unjust death of a just man vindicated by God, speaking to every other act of injustice and putting it into a new light. The Father has taken the side of Jesus against human injustice in raising him from the dead.

Every time we celebrate the Eucharist, we celebrate the justice of God over against the human injustice which killed Christ and continues on its death-dealing way among us in the present. By celebrating the Eucharist, we align ourselves with Christ and rejoice in the Father, who is the *source of*:

our *hope* for justice,

our *faith* that there can be justice,

a *love* which seeks to bring about justice.

This means that we seek to bring about justice and we seek to open our world to the presence of the God whose rule will give justice a home in the world. This reign of God was proclaimed by Jesus before people who would have been happy with revenge on the Romans, with prosperity and ease, with the satisfaction of their immediate needs. He did it before the opposition of Jewish leaders to a reign of God stretching out to all. He did it before his own disciples disillusioned by his lack of concern for their own places in his kingdom. He did it before a Roman governor from whom he accepted judgment rather than be unfaithful to his Father, in whom he placed his hope for justice (judgment).

Our alignment with Jesus in the Eucharist draws us into the thrust of his life, and into trust in the Father's justice. But in this, Jesus himself had to struggle with the frustration of his mission and the injustice that was worked upon him. He, like so many other human beings before and after him, caught in the injustice of the world, had to work through the meaning and fulfilment of his life before God his Father. He had to come to believe that humanity had not been left abandoned to its fate or left to the changing winds of chance; but in fact can rely on the God who is trustworthy and to whom those who are unjustly dealt with are dear. This God has become poor and disregarded beside them in Jesus Christ our Lord, *out of* whose *life* we live and whose *death* we seek to live *out*.

Having looked at the reality of memorial in this chapter, we will now move on to look at the action which Jesus left us to do in his memorial – what it is that he commanded us to do.

Reflection

1. Find examples of the workings of memorial in your own life. Do these help you to understand the Eucharist?

2. What is your understanding of the meaning of 'living out' and 'living out of' the death and resurrection of Jesus?

3. How important is the centrality of the question of justice in Christian living?

3 | *The last supper and the Eucharist*

What Jesus gave us

'Do this in memory of me.' The 'this' in this phrase of the institution narrative is the Jewish ritual meal which Jesus celebrated with his disciples. There is considerable disagreement among scholars as to whether or not it was a passover meal but it certainly was a ritual meal. It is presented in a passover setting by the New Testament.[15]

The fact that we are dealing with a ritual meal is important. This determines the form of our memorial communion with Jesus: it occurs in the ingestion of food and drink in a meal. This is the symbolic form of our communion with Christ, that is, this form leads us to discover the nature of the relationship we have with Jesus, the nature of the communion established between ourselves and Jesus before the Father.

The use of food means that we are dealing with one of the deepest forms of symbolism known to humanity. When we consume food, it becomes us, it constitutes our bodily being. This is a union deeper than that imaged in sexual union, or in the communion established by words. It is concrete and bodily and constitutive of our very selves.

It is this human and religious activity – eating a meal – that forms our mode of communion with Jesus before his Father. This symbolic form suggests the nature and depth of that relationship.

The characteristics of meal as a human reality shed light on our eucharistic relationship with Jesus. And since the Eucharist is the ritual in which we discover our identity as Christians, the symbolic form of the meal is an element in the formation of our identity. It is by means of this specific human reality that we enter into the eucharistic process by which we come to belong to the Church. It is the ritual means of the Church's self-expression and establishment.

The last supper

In Christ's memory we are commanded to do in our Eucharists what he did at the last supper. This is a particular form of the ritual of a meal.

To explain the relationship between our Eucharists and the last supper I would like to borrow some very useful terminology from an Italian theologian, Enrico Mazza, which he in turn takes from the works of the philosopher and historian, Umberto Eco.[16]

This terminology sees the last supper as the *code* we use to decipher the meaning of the Eucharist. We use codes regularly. The telegraph uses Morse code combining short and long sounds to communicate words. To understand its message, we must know the code which links the sounds to words. The telegraph embodies this code. Likewise, language uses a code to make human sounds communicative: it has an alphabet, syntax and grammar. We cannot receive this communication without knowing the code. Football games have codes – rugby, soccer, Australian or Irish football. We must know the codes to be able to participate and we cannot change codes as we play, nor can we mix codes.

In each of these cases the code is being acted out in the activity. It is by means of it that these activities achieve their purpose: the code enables the telegraph to communicate, a language to be spoken, a football game to be played. It is the foundation of these various human activities, enabling a transition to take place, or activity to go forward.

Thus we can describe the last supper as the code which is internal to and operative in the Eucharist. It is the internal meaning-bearing code which enables us to say that we do now what Jesus did at the last supper. Thus, we identify our activity in the Eucharist. It gives meaning to the action, it enables the Eucharist to function just as the code of the football game does for each particular game.

If we did not know of the last supper, the action of the Eucharist would have some other meaning. To describe this a little differently, we overlay the image of the last supper on the Eucharist and allow their convergences to become apparent, to lock into each other. This reveals to us what the Eucharist is; it identifies its core.

Looking at the last supper we can say that it is wholly explained as a way of referring to the pending death of Jesus. It is not a reality in and of itself but it is a reference to, and a function of, the death of Jesus.

The last supper refers the loaf of bread and the cup of wine to the death of Jesus and to the participating group's relationship to that death. This action and these words stretch out towards the next day's events in such a way that they are inexplicable without those events. Because the last supper has this character, our Eucharist takes on this reference as well. St Paul, (1 Cor 10:16), already builds into the Lord's supper this reference back to Christ's death. Precisely from the community's post-resurrection perspective, Paul says: 'Is not this bread we break a participation in the body of Christ?; Is not the cup we bless a participation in the blood of Christ?'.

All the terms used are references to the death of Jesus and they interpret that death in biblical imagery: 'body given', 'blood of the covenant', 'for you and for all'. This code is built into our Eucharist. It is our participation in the passover of Jesus through death to the Father. We do now what Jesus did then.

Eucharist: sacrament of the Lord's supper

In the Eucharist the Church does not repeat, or imitate, or dramatically present, what happened at the last supper. Rather, the Eucharist is the extension or actuation of the last supper, the sacrament of Christ now present in his Church doing what he did at the last supper, that is, giving himself over to the Father for the coming of the Father's reign upon us. Jesus' action at the last supper he now embodies in the action of his Church as it does what he commands in his memory.

St John Chrysostom helps us to understand this.[17] He sees Christ's command to do this in memory of him as parallel to God's command to Adam and Eve to increase and multiply and fill the earth. When a couple obeys this command, God's blessing is actuated in them. So it is with the Eucharist: each time we obey Christ's command, what he did at the last supper is actuated among us. As 'increase and multiply' was said once and is forever operative, so Christ's command was said once but is operative in each Eucharist celebrated. The Eucharist is the sacrament of the Lord's supper.

This also highlights the important point that the Eucharist is Christ's activity. It is Christ who is at work when we do now what he did then. This is the action of Christ in the community of his disciples as they do the Eucharist in his memory. We will need to return to this point when we consider the relationship of the community and its presider.

The Eucharist is the sacrament of the whole supper

The Eucharist is based on the whole ritual of the last supper, not just the recorded words of Jesus. The full ritual of the Eucharist from the preparation of the gifts through the Eucharistic Prayer to the Communion rite is our doing now what Jesus did. Our tendency to isolate the institution narrative impedes an adequate understanding of the Eucharist. The words 'take-bless-break-give' were, and are, technical terms to describe the actions of the ritual meal and so of the Eucharist. This whole action is the origin of the eucharistic liturgy, not the institution narrative as such.

What the first Christians did was to do what Jesus did. The function of the institution narrative was not to constitute the Eucharist but to give expression to its code: the last supper. By it, Christians knew the meaning of this action they were doing, thirty or forty or fifty years after the death of Jesus. The account of the last supper narrated in the institution narrative was their checkpoint; it showed them what their action meant and consequently who they were. Its origin is in fact illustrated in St Paul's introduction to his account of the institution of the Eucharist. He reprimands the Corinthians for their misuse of the

Lord's supper, their failure to recognise what it really meant. He then gives them his account of the Eucharist's origins to show them its true meaning:

> Now that I am on the subject of instructions, I cannot say that you have done well in holding meetings that do you more harm than good. In the first place, I hear that when you all come together as a community, there are separate factions among you, and I half believe it – since there must no doubt be separate groups among you, to distinguish those who are to be trusted. The point is, when you hold these meetings, it is not the Lord's supper that you are eating, since when the time comes to eat, everyone is in such a hurry to start his own supper that one person goes hungry while another is getting drunk. Surely you have homes for eating and drinking in? Surely you have enough respect for the community of God not to make poor people embarrassed? What am I to say to you? Congratulate you? I cannot congratulate you on this. For this is what I received from the Lord, and in turn passed on to you: that on the same night that he was betrayed, the Lord Jesus took some bread, and thanked God for it and broke it, and he said, 'This is my body, which is for you; do this as a memorial of me.' In the same way he took the cup after supper, and said, 'This cup is the new covenant in my blood. Whenever you drink it, do this as a memorial of me.' Until the Lord comes, therefore, every time you eat this bread and drink this cup, you are proclaiming his death, and so anyone who eats the bread or drinks the cup of the Lord unworthily will be behaving unworthily towards the body and blood of the Lord. (1 Cor 11:17-27)

This illustrates the purpose of the institution narrative in the Eucharist: to tell us the meaning of the reality we are celebrating in the whole liturgy of the Eucharist. It is a miniature of the whole, and explicitly expresses the present Church's rootedness in the action of Jesus and the significance of the Church's present eucharistic action.

We will discuss later the place and role of the institution narrative in the structure of the Eucharistic Prayer. For the moment, let us say that the institution narrative expresses the link between our action and that of Christ, the fact that we are summoned and gathered to this action by him, that we are dependent upon him.

What the institution narrative says of the Eucharist is true, what it says of the bread and wine taken up in the eucharistic action is true. But it is describing the whole, not indicating a single moment in the eucharistic celebration.

One of the ways in which the early Fathers of the Church talked about the Eucharist was as 'the image and likeness' of the last supper.[18] They did not pray that the bread and wine become the body and blood of Christ but that the Father see in this action of the Church 'the image and likeness' of the action of Christ at the last supper. We might put this in words reminiscent of the present Third Eucharistic Prayer of the *Roman Missal*, which asks the Father to look upon the action of the Church, and to see the action of Christ.[19] In its earliest versions, The *Roman Canon* would seem to have been cast in this 'image and likeness' form.[20]

This understanding of the Eucharist is based on the awareness that Christ is present in the whole of the Church's eucharistic action from its beginning to its end (take-bless-break-give). The presence of Christ is given communicable form for us in its concretisation in the bread and wine taken up into the eucharistic action. By this the Christ who is doing now in the Eucharist what he did at the last supper takes us up into his action by our communion with him. By that communion we are taken up into him, he is not enclosed within us.

We can compare this to a football game, in which the whole action is concentrated in what is done with the ball. So the whole action of the Eucharist is concerned with what is done with bread and wine, which give us communion with Christ and his action in the Eucharist. It gives his presence such a form – that of food – that we can take it into us, making us the Body of Christ, the Church.

We return to a crucial point. The Eucharist does not have as its purpose, the presence of Christ in bread and wine but his presence in his body, the Church. This presence is achieved in and through the transformed bread and wine. The mentality we have received in recent centuries concentrates so much upon the presence of Christ in the bread and wine that it loses the sense of the Eucharist's full meaning, namely the unity of Christ and his disciples in his body, the Church, achieved by means of the eucharistic presence of Christ in and through the bread and wine.

The Eucharist belongs to the whole community

The Eucharist is, of its nature, the celebration of the whole community of the Church, the means by which the Church's very unity and identity are established. In the Eucharist, the Church becomes that communion of life in Christ which it receives in the Eucharistic bread and wine, identified with Christ in his passover to the Father.

This requires some reflection on the relationship between the whole community of the Church and one of its members who presides over the celebration of the Eucharist. In the Catholic tradition, the presider means the bishop or the priest.

We have inherited from the middle ages a mentality which assumes that the priest is the real celebrant of the Mass. The community attends what the priest does. As we recognise the presence of this presumed mentality among us we are impelled to re-think the presiding minister's role and his place within the community of the Church. This inherited mentality saw the priest doing what Christ did in an exclusive sense, while the community was seen as present to receive this mystery.

This mentality is diminishing in many parts of the Church but it has a strong unreflective hold in the recent Catholic mind and if we probe our spontaneous attitudes we might find it lurking more strongly than we imagine. It is extremely important to re-think this issue if the Church as a whole is to take greater possession of its identity and mission, if we are to remember more accurately who we are. This inherited mentality effectively throws into question the common priesthood of all the faithful as they are seen too easily as participating in the Eucharist only in a receptive way.

The bishop or priest presides at the Eucharist precisely because the Eucharist is the action of the whole Church. New Testament evidence points to the practice of the leader of the community celebrating the Eucharist precisely as the leader of the community.[21] Because the Eucharist is an action of the community as a whole it is led by the community's leader. Leadership of the Eucharist devolves from leadership of the community.

A strong element in the consciousness of the early Church was that the Eucharist was an act of the community of the Church as such. It was the place where Christians expressed and found reinforced their very identity as Christians, what later theology would call the source and summit of the Church's life.

Because of the many and varied practices in the celebration of the Eucharist in the intervening centuries, this sense of the unity of the Church and Eucharist has slackened in the awareness of the Church – both at the level of common awareness and at the level of official documents.

So strong was this awareness in the first Christian centuries that when in Rome, a city with a large population, there had to be more than the one Eucharist, with the bishop the link between the Eucharist, presided over by the bishop, and the Eucharists presided over by the presbyters in other parts of the city was expressed ritually in the presbyter-led celebrations. Writing this into the celebrations ritually was writing this link into the very identity of those communities celebrating under the leadership of the presbyters.

This ritual was the rite of the fermentum whose pale reflection exists still in the contemporary celebration of the Mass. A particle of the host from the Eucharist at which the bishop was presiding was sent to the Eucharistic assembly at which the presbyter was presiding and was dropped into the chalice at that celebration. This rite signified that it was the same mystery of ecclesial union with Christ which was being celebrated at both Eucharists, that is, that those gathered at both places were drawn into the one Body of Christ.[22] Our contemporary practice of placing a part of the host into the chalice after the Fraction has its origin in this practice.

The leader of any community is the sign of its unity and identity. It is in the acknowledgment of this leadership that a community finds its social unity which is bound up intrinsically with the community's identity because it involves agreement – even if implicit – about the nature of the community.

Since the core of the Church's identity involves its relationship to Christ, all of those things which enter into that identity such as its central rituals, its leadership structures, came to be understood in terms of different ways in which Christ relates to his Church. In this is the development of the theology of the sacraments, including that of Orders.

As time went on an understanding of the leadership structures of the Church and so of the leadership of the Eucharist developed and a theology of episcopacy and presbyterate emerged. This was a complex development and was influenced by the forms and understanding of leadership in the various cultures and historical periods in which it took place.[23] I would like to mention two perspectives that continue to provide a balanced and rich understanding of these ministries as serving the priesthood of the whole Church.

Firstly, as already noted, leadership of the Eucharist devolves from leadership of the community. This makes leadership of the Eucharist thoroughly ecclesial. It is the leader of the community who seals this celebration as being truly 'of the community', 'of the Church'. The leader is witness and assurance that this is an act of the Church. The priest or bishop, by their presence and leadership enables the ritual of the Eucharist to be an ecclesial act. According to the 'ordering' of the community, they are the focus of the Church's unity and identity, and because the Eucharist is the ritual of this unity and identity, their leadership is required. From the early Middle Ages the ordination rites began to express an understanding of ordination in terms of the conferring of power to offer sacrifice over against the earlier understanding in terms of the ordering or structuring of the community of the Church.[24]

The ordering of the community of the Church (or establishing its structure of leadership) reflects the way in which any human group must act if it is to maintain itself and flourish. The Christian faith is essentially a communal and not an individual reality and so has to face the struggles that all human groups experience in keeping themselves in unity. So the structuring of the Church is not extrinsic to its nature and mission but is part of its nature as a human reality which is also involved in God's plan. Its structures are a part of the way in which the Pentecostal Spirit works against the forces of Babel which are part of the Church as a human reality.

A leadership structure has developed to take in the universal/local polarity of the Catholic Church. The ministries of bishop and presbyter are ministries of unity and so they form the links between the various manifestations of the Church. The presbyter is leader of the local community of the Church which gathers in its own place (e.g. the parish) and at the same time is part of the presbyteral body around the bishop. The bishop in turn is leader of the full local Church, a particular Church within the universal Church (the diocese), while at the same time being a member of the episcopal college whose leader is the Bishop of Rome, the pope. These ministries are about unity on this larger scale and the presiding of these leaders at the Eucharist bespeaks the nature of the Eucharist as belonging not only to the locally gathered community of the Church but also to the Church as a worldwide communion of communities (or communions) which is the universal Church.

The second important perspective I would like to suggest is that from early on in the development of the tradition a particular relationship came to be discerned between the role of the presiding minister of the Eucharist and the role of Christ in the Church. The bishop or presbyter came to be seen as a sign of Christ, not as a matter of personal holiness or of the effectiveness of the ministry of the person but in terms of the role fulfilled by the person. That is, in terms of the position of the person in the 'ordering' or structuring of the Church, and out of this grew a theology of 'holy orders'.

The presiding minister is the focus of unity in the gathering of the community of the Church and in the structural or ordering sense is a sign of Christ who is the one who gathers us together to hear his word and to celebrate his Eucharist. But the gathering takes place within and by means of a sign-system of which the leader of the gathered community is a part. The action of the Eucharist is a symbolic activity in which human persons, human words and human objects become the means of reaching beyond what we can see, hear and touch to the Christ who presents himself to us now as he did to his original disciples at the last supper.

Within that symbolic activity (or sign system) the leader of the community does those things and says those things which specifically relate to the actions and words of Christ. Thus the leader of the community is the sign of Christ transcendentally present within his Body, the Church. These leaders are signs of Christ as focus points of the Church's unity and identity and they are signs of Christ in so far as they 'sit in the Chair of the Lord' when the community of the Church gathers to do what Jesus did on the night before he died. This symbolic nature of the eucharistic action explains why it is the presiding minister who prays the Eucharistic Prayer and does the other actions specific to Christ at the last supper.

The eucharistic action is that of Christ done now by the Church but it is his action which we now do, and into which we are being drawn. It is his handing over of himself to the Father into which we are being caught up. So in accord with the symbolic character of the action, it is the bishop or priest who prays the Eucharistic Prayer as the prayer of Christ. We affirm our willingness and commitment to become one with Christ, which unity is given to us in the action of Communion.

The ministry of the person who presides is a ministry of the community. It expresses something which is integral to the community's own identity, giving symbolic form to a dimension of the community's own nature. The Eucharistic Prayer is not, therefore, the priest's prayer but the community's prayer prayed by the priest because of the very nature of the community as a group already in communion with Christ – but not yet! They are becoming the Body of Christ.

The Fathers of the Church see the Eucharistic Prayers as radically communal. The priest, as he begins the Eucharistic Prayer, presents himself before the people to receive from them the licence to go ahead with the prayer. He says, 'The Lord be with you'; they reply: 'And also with you'; he: 'Lift up your hearts', they: 'We have lifted them up to the Lord'; he: 'Let us give thanks to the Lord our God', they: 'It is right to give him thanks and praise'. In this John Chrysostom sees the unity of priest and people being expressed:

> In the celebration of the wonderful Mysteries, the priest certainly prays for the people, but the people also pray for

the priest; for the words 'And with your spirit' have no other meaning. The Eucharist is equally common to them for it is not the priest alone who gives thanks but the whole people. Actually it is after he has received the assent of the faithful and after they have agreed that it is right and just that the priest begins the Thanksgiving.[25]

St Augustine speaks of the *'habemus ad Dominum'* (we have lifted them up to the Lord) as that which stirs the president to follow through with the thanksgiving.[26]

The 'Great Amen' corresponds to these phrases of the initial dialogue. It is the formal signature of the people corresponding to their licensing of the priest at the beginning of the Eucharistic Prayer to speak in their name. They have fulfilled the Lord's command – a charge given to the whole community of the Church. They seal this with the final 'Amen'. Within this action of the Church, the presider or priest has a clear, specific role, but he is a minister to the action to which the whole community is summoned by Christ.

In the next chapter we will continue to look at the Eucharist from the point of view of what Jesus left us to celebrate, but from a different perspective. We will examine the Eucharist in terms of:

- the symbolism of meal,
- its being a ritual,
- its specific nature as a ritual with Christian meaning.

Reflection

1. The Eucharist needs to be seen as a communal act. Can this be reconciled with the strong individualism in our culture?

2. Why is there a need for the development of new ministries in the Church?

3. How would you see the Eucharist celebrated in the future?

4 | *A meal*

Doing what Jesus did involves using a particular ritual or symbolic activity which is given to us by Jesus at the origin of our tradition. What he gave us on the night before he died was already a human, religious and cultural activity used by the Jewish people to express their identity and their relationship to God in the covenant of Sinai. It already carried meaning; it already had a structure. By Jesus' use of it and by our Christian use of it in memory of Jesus, it has gathered further meaning and undergone structural development. Even though there has been change, we still seek to structure the shape of our contemporary Eucharist on the fundamental actions with bread and wine which Jesus did at the Last Supper – take, bless, break, give – actions Jewish fathers and leaders had done for centuries before him.

It is significant that we are using the form of a meal as our symbolic form, because it presupposes the suitability of its symbolism for what we are celebrating through it, and that in the working out of the ways of our tradition, this form has emerged as the one that most suitably offers itself as an expression of the Christian mystery of union with Jesus. In the gradual working out of the ways of any religious tradition some things fit the tradition better than others, or find better response within the tradition. These things are central to its identity.

In a work on the praise (or liturgy) of Israel, Walter Brueggeman says:

> I submit that the work of the people in liturgy is to process shared experience through the normative narratives, images, metaphors and symbols of that community. Shared experience from one community is not unlike experience that is found in other communities. What is distinctive is the range of symbols through which the experience is processed.'[27]

This is precisely the point I would like to make. Christians process human experience through Jesus' life, death and resurrection. They also have symbolic activities and rituals, called sacraments, through which they filter that processing of their experience. Pivotal to all of these rituals is the Eucharist whose symbolic form is meal. What Christians were given as a means of communion in God were not pilgrimages, or prayer exercises, or feats of penance, but the symbolic form of meal as shaped by Israel's experience of it. What is distinctive for Christians is Christ, and, at the ritual level, the pivotal symbol of meal as the means of communication and communion with Christ.

Therefore the characteristics of meal have their influence in processing the shared experience of Christians. This symbolic form influences the distinctive shape of Christianity. So we need to look at the characteristics of this form to know about the Christian faith.

According to the *Roman Missal*, the first part of the celebration of the Liturgy of the Eucharist – the preparation of the gifts – corresponds to Jesus' action in taking bread and wine; the second part – the Eucharistic

Prayer – to his action of blessing God over them; and the third part – the communion rite – to his action of breaking bread and giving it, and of giving the cup to be shared. We do what he did in the liturgical structure of the Mass.[28]

This action of Jesus taken up by the Church has layers of meaning that we need to unfold if we are to appreciate the specific theology of the Eucharist, which emerges from the combination and interaction of the paschal mystery of Jesus and the meaning of meal as a human reality, permeated by the theology and spirituality of Israel and then as a reality taken up by Jesus and related to his death.

Meal is the 'symbol' we are given for the discovery of Christ's presence among us and for the development of our understanding of that presence. A symbol is not there to veil but, in its difference, to reveal; that is, in the difference between itself and Christ present among us, we discover likenesses which help us to see the faith-filled celebration of the Eucharist as an activity in which we discover Christ present. So we seek to reflect on the meaning of the meal as a human reality and let that flow into our understanding of the Eucharist.

Meal as symbol in human life

Meals, the taking of food together, are a central reality of human life, and take different forms in different cultures. What I am about to present comes out of European culture with its biblical-Christian back-ground. Many of the elements I will present are common to all cultures; some are neglected in different periods of the development of any culture; some are neglected in contemporary western culture.

Meals are human activities which gather people together. There are times when members of a group or family, who do many different things during their days, come together to eat, and in that many other things happen – there is personal encounter, talk, a sense of being together. It is a simple activity and yet it is also complex. All that comprises this group of people is potentially brought into the gathering. It is an activity which takes a lot of preparation, absorbs a large proportion of the resources of the group. The energy expended by the breadwinners in the family or group provides the bread – food for the table at which the whole group will gather. It draws together the lives of these people not only in the visible reality of their sitting together, but in many subtle ways.

Meals are firstly and most obviously about food, and food is about life. If we do not eat, our life drains away from us: we are dependent on food for life. We are dependent on something outside of ourselves to maintain our own existence. The very fact that we eat food is a statement that we are not self-sufficient, we do not have our own source of life within ourselves. It does not matter how autonomous we think we are, our need for food reminds us emphatically that we live in dependence on something else. Our need for food has always been a sign of the life-giver for human beings. In many religions food – and especially the basic, staple food – is used in the worship of gods. It has been perceived constantly by human beings as the sign of our dependence for life on a greater giver of life. Although we all recognise our dependence on food, the way human beings read this as a sign can differ. In the Eucharist we proclaim Jesus as bread for us. He is true bread bringing life, doing the work even better than bread does it!

This life we take into ourselves in food which comes from the earth. We live in a universe which is nourishing, which has within itself the power to give life. The earth is our mother and, as we eat, we are in a sense feeding from her breasts. We, in our own day, have experienced something of the threat that human beings know in famine: what will happen if our earth has its nourishing capacity threatened by environmental pollution? Food is our basic link to the earth; in her food products, she enters into us. We are of the same substance as the earth. We are of the earth. There is a deep solidarity with all of creation in our taking in of food.

This solidarity is not lost in the Eucharist. Jesus was in solidarity with the earth through the fruits of it which fed his body. In turn, our earth was glorified in his truly glorified humanity. As the fruits of the earth are taken up into the Eucharist to be the means of our communion with Jesus, they are transformed by their relationship to him, as human flesh was transformed in his resurrection from death. Our earthliness is now taken into a new relationship which gives it a future in the glory of the risen Lord.

Food also involves a solidarity with people, not just in the meal where we eat together, but in the fact that most of our food is not the direct product of nature, but nature taken up into a human activity in which it becomes transformed into our food by preparation, cooking, and garnishing. For our very bread we are dependent on those who make it out of grain, which we cannot use as food without the many steps needed to transform it from grain to bread. In our contemporary culture in industrialised societies, the processes of producing, delivering and preparing food requires an enormous cooperative effort. We are dependent on so many others for suitable food to eat. Food production has always created human togetherness and co-operation and has absorbed huge amounts of human energy. It has often been the very basis of the division of labour in human societies. Producing food for the table effectively brings about human solidarity.

Food is taken into us physically, and becomes our very physical substance. We might say that we become what we eat. This is very significant because it poses a relationship between us and our food which is similar to, and yet quite different from, what was said above about food giving us life. When we hold food which we are about to eat we are saying in this action, 'this is my body', because that is what it is about to become. There is a great concreteness in this: there is a relationship between food and our body. This is the basis for that dimension of food symbolism which is open to the greatest intensity of interiorisation between us and another created thing: nothing else becomes us as food does. The closest to it is our being constituted by substances from our parents' bodies. This is crucial for our understanding of the Eucharist. As we participate in the Eucharist, it is the symbolic form of a meal which provides the imagery which will guide us into our understanding of the communion between us and Jesus.

Food is shared in a meal. This is one of the dimensions of food symbolism most taken into the awareness of Israel in its sense of meals taken together. When we eat the one piece of food – bread, a piece of meat, etc – we divide that food so that all who are at the table may share in the one piece of food; that is, so that all will draw life and be constituted in their very bodiliness by the one shared piece of food. It is the original single piece of food which ends up in the bodies of many thus drawing them into a common unity. The breaking of the one loaf is very signficant: the fact that it is broken and shared means that this act is a fundamental sign of unity. It functioned thus as a sign in Israel and among many other peoples.

This is already an expression of human unity, of a sharing of life, of fellowship, of welcome. There is a certain instinctiveness in our sharing a meal with people: when we meet people we share food together. As we get to know people better, we are invited to eat with them as a sign of welcome into their homes and their lives: it bespeaks a solidarity and a sharing of our futures, even a sense of commitment to them.

The meal does what its central action signs in other ways. It is not just in the sharing of bread that all of this takes place. Gathering for the sharing of bread, we enter into conversation, interaction; we come to know each other, to achieve through words and attentiveness to each other what is symbolised and what happens physically in the sharing of food.

There is a certain power in this action of gathering at the table; it invokes in us a movement towards personal interaction. Let me give an example of this 'power' of the table. If you go into a cafeteria alone and cannot find a spare table, you face the prospect of sharing a table with someone you do not know. Sitting at the table, you can experience a tension: do I acknowledge this other person and at least say something to him or her or do I pretend the person is not there and go on with my eating having created a psychic wall between us? This is a tension created by sitting at table with other people. It is the 'power' of the table at work. Eating at the same table, even in this form, evokes in us the memory of what eating at table can be and naturally seeks to be.

The table is often a central object in the home, occupying a central place in a particular room. All the other objects in the room are oriented towards it. Some objects are used to prepare the food to be eaten at the table; there are chairs to sit on at the table and cupboards containing the implements to be used at the table.

As we shall see, all of this symbolism flows over into the Eucharist. The Eucharist is the one loaf which makes us the one body (1 Cor 10:16). There are liturgical and theological implications of this symbolism. The meal gives us a wonderful image of the Eucharist as the gathering of the disciples of Jesus into unity with him and each other.

Meal in Israel

The Old Testament used the symbol of the meal in its own religious culture. As a symbol it unearths and brings to light characteristics of that culture. Israel used meals religiously in the home, but also within the temple area where particular groups could celebrate fellowship meals, and as part of certain sacrificial activities such as the commmunion sacrifice.[29] There were meals at the great feasts, among which the Passover meal was predominant. The sabbath meal was celebrated each week.

The structure used in these meals varied with occasions and according to particular customs and during various periods of Israel's history. Scholars are increasingly aware that they cannot make too many presumptions, from later texts, about the period before the rabbinic organisation of Israel's customs following the destruction of the state of Israel and the temple by the Romans.[30]

We can presume that the basic structure at the beginning of the meal followed this pattern: bread taken, God blessed, bread broken and given to all by the father of the family or the leader of the group. This action constituted the table fellowship, after which the meal took place. This was usually quite simple but on occasions like Passover could contain various symbolic elements. At the end of the meal, a cup of wine would be taken, at least on festive occasions, and God would be blessed over it. It was to be shared or each would drink from their own cup. On an occasion like Passover several cups would be drunk. This basic structure would be at work whenever the ritual meal was celebrated.[31] A theology developed around several elements in this structure.

Bread

Bread is the primordial sign of God. As the staple food, it becomes the symbolic food to which great significance is attached. It gives life just as God gives life. It gives life which comes from the life-giver. It does the work of the creator. It does a job which is God's alone to do: give life. This creates a link between bread and God which makes it natural to use bread as the gift over which we bless God. The recogniton of God at work happens in bread and so, we acknowledge God over this gift of it, as we perceive and recognise God at work giving life through it. It is not just that God established this quality in bread in the past; rather, God is at work now in bread as it gives us life.

There is a covenant with the earth in this. God has made the earth fruitful, producing bread (and wine) because of God's blessing. This is, so to speak, the first layer of God's covenantal relationship with the People of God and with all people.

Bread is used to bless God for other life-giving activities. The other gifts of God to the people such as freedom-giving deliverance from salvery in Egypt and the life-giving covenant are related to the fundamental gift of bread, extensions of bread as God's basic blessing. The God who gives life in bread gives life through the exodus and the covenant. So God is blessed over bread for these other 'blessings', because they have a similarity to bread, God's primordial gift. Bread becomes the sign of all these other life-giving blessings because of its original nature. So it is used in the feast of Passover as well as the Lamb, the bitter herbs, etc.

Blessing

Blessing is one of Israel's most basic religious attitudes. It means acknowledgment, recognition issuing in praise, done over a gift of God in which God is acknowledged to be at work blessing. So to bless God is a movement on our part towards God.

In this act of blessing we open ourselves to God's blessing the flow of which continues. By our act of acknowledgment we open ourselves to continue to receive God's blessing. God continues to bless us as we bless God.[32] This blessing of God is based on our remembering God, and in remembering, we recognise God and God's blessing.

Forgetfulness is the source of non-belief in Israel; it involves the non-recognition that all comes from God. To bless God is to live in the flow of God's blessing us. So blessing God for the gift of the exodus and the covenant at passover time, is to put oneself in the current of that gift and to praise God for delivering 'us and our ancestors' out of the slavery of Egypt.

Breaking bread

In Judaism, the breaking of the bread is a technical term for the action which begins the ritual meal and which constitutes the group participating in this communion or fellowship. It is the core act of the Jewish domestic ritual,[33] used to describe the whole action of which it is the beginning. It is understood that the people who gather for this action and the meal which follows are gathered into a communion and fellowship of life, seen as being in solidarity with each other. Indeed, it is ascertained before the meal if there are any immovable obstacles to this solidarity (e.g. ritual uncleanness). The table is not open to anyone and everyone; the participants' unity with each other is presupposed. As we saw earlier, all of this is implied in the very nature of the meal as a human reality. It is considered an offence to betray the people at table with you, as evidenced in the lament: 'Even my closest and most trusted friend, who shared my table, rebels against me.'(Ps 41:9) The people gathered at table are united to God in their common act of receiving God's gifts together.

Wine

Wine has a different significance to bread in Israel's religious culture. Bread is the staple food associated with every meal. Wine is a festive food associated with feasting, with the letting go of controls, with abundance, with life overflowing. It represents good gifts received and yet to come: the abundance and joy of *shalom*. It lends itself therefore to talk about God's kingdom, where there will be joy and festival and abundance. All these elements of meals in Israel are used as ways of entering into communion in God's blessings which is what the meal is always about although different feasts and occasions may emphasise God's different blessings.

Meal in the New Testament

This inherited religious act of Israel is naturally a part of the life of Jesus the Jew. It is something he does in his family, on the feasts of Israel and in the ordinary circumstances of his life. Moving around Israel on his mission from the Father, he is doing it as a natural part of his life with his disciples and with people he meets.

The New Testament reports meals of Jesus[34] and also offers reflection on their place in his life and that of his earliest followers.[35] Given that the New Testament was written from the standpoint of a post-resurrection belief in the risen Lord these passages also reflect the place of the new ritual meal in the life of the early Church, which, in writing about meals in the life of Jesus projects images of its participation in the Lord's supper or the breaking of the bread, or the authentic bread from heaven. The narratives of the multiplication of the loaves, and meals with Jesus after his resurrection, have their importance in this regard.

There are three key points to make about meals in Jesus' own life:

1. There were occasions of considerable conflict in his life when he ate with people whom the Jewish leaders considered to be beyond the pale. The dynamic of solidarity and communion naturally involved in the meal meant that as Jesus ate with publicans and sinners, he entered into communion with them and this was a cause of conflict with the protectors of Israel's traditions. As the New Testament looks back on these as actions of the Lord, whom they have discovered more deeply, these meals appear as the

beginning of his new covenant in which God is reaching out to sinners. In these meals the salvation God is offering the people in Jesus is already being offered and accepted.

2. As Jesus' own disciples continue to eat with him, they are aligned with him by the very dynamics of the meal. They are putting themselves into solidarity with him by their continued meals and thereby into a position of alienation from those who take their distance from Jesus. They participate in the fate towards which Jesus is moving, and this will become a clear feature of the understanding of the Eucharist.

3. Highly significant is the meal which Jesus shares with his disciples 'on the night before he dies'. Whatever the dispute about whether the last supper was the passover meal or some other kind of meal, scholars agree that such a meal took place.[36] It is presented to us in the synoptic gospels as integral to the passion of Jesus and as the basis of the Church's later practice of the Lord's supper or the breaking of the bread. It is, therefore, important that we look into the presentation of this meal in the New Testament narratives of the institution of the Eucharist.

The institution narratives of the Eucharist

The institution narratives present to us an event in which Jesus engages in the ritual meal he has inherited from Israel.[37] He is presented as doing this on the night before he dies and in a passover context which is explicit in the synoptics but is not mentioned in Paul. Jesus is presented as removing this religious act from its reference to God mediated by the exodus and its covenant, and making of it a reference to his own death by which a new covenant is established with his Father.

These narratives present the supper as being about the death of Jesus.

Xavier Léon-Dufour in his book *Sharing the Eucharistic Bread* suggests that what happened on the night before Jesus died comes to us in two traditions: one *cultic*, the ritual meal of the supper, and the other *testamentary*, a farewell meal during which Jesus gives us his last will and testament. This latter we see in John's discourses at the last supper and in Luke.[38]

The cultic tradition has two forms – one usually described as Antiochene and represented by the related narratives of Luke and Paul and the other Marcan, represented by Mark and Matthew's narratives of the institution.[39]

I do not intend to offer a detailed exegesis of these narratives, but I refer the reader to the many works dealing with them.[40]

I propose to consider the narratives in a general way by looking at the basic meaning given to this act of Jesus by the symbols used to draw out this meaning and by the context in which it is placed.

The last supper meal is placed by all New Testament writers, either explicitly (Paul) or by context (synoptics) on the night before Jesus dies. It is his last act with his disciples before his death separates him from them. It is seen as a part of the movement towards his death since it is placed within the passion narratives by Mark, Matthew and Luke.

Eschatological

There is an eschatological perspective on the part of Jesus as he celebrates the supper. This is strong in Luke:

When the hour came he took his place at table and the apostles with him. And he said to them, 'I have longed to eat this passover with you before I suffer; because I tell you, I shall not eat it again until it is fulfilled in the kingdom of God.' Then,taking a cup, he gave thanks and said, 'Take this and share it among you, because from now on, I tell you, I shall not drink wine until the kingdom of God comes.' (22:14-18)

Then follows the institution narrative of the Eucharist. But this perspective is also present in Mark after the institution of the Eucharist: 'I tell you solemnly, I shall not drink any more wine until the day I drink new wine in the kingdom of God'. (14:25) Matthew has a very similar formula to Mark's (see Mt 26:29).

This eschatological perspective puts the death of Jesus and the supper which is related to it in the perspective of God's kingdom which has been the driving force of Jesus' whole life. These words relate what Jesus is now doing to the future coming of that kingdom and puts his death into that perspective.

Passover

The gospels emphasise the passover context of the last supper which, in the synoptics, occurs during a passover meal for which the disciples had earlier been sent to prepare (Mk 14:12-16; Mt 26:17-19; Lk 22:7-13). John's supper on the night before the death of Jesus, though it has no institution narrative, is given a strong passover setting by the words of introduction: 'Before the festival of the passover, Jesus knew that his hour had come to pass from this world to the Father. Having loved those who were his own in the world, he loved them to the end. They were at supper ...' (Jn 13:1-2).

The passover context is important for appreciating the early Christian understanding of the last supper and Jesus' death. It is saying that this is the new passover, that Jesus' death is the new exodus, and that in all of this there is a new covenant. This is a radical claim whose consequences will be teased out only gradually. The supper held with his disciples before his death, is to be done as a memorial, just as the Israelites had a meal on the eve of their departure from Egypt as a memorial of that event.

Dialogical

The last supper is an act which takes place within the relationship of Jesus and his disciples. He is presented as the active one in the whole action but all he does presumes response from the disciples: their taking, their eating, their drinking. It is something going on between him and them. It is important for us to understand this dialogical structure to the action of the supper. Léon-Dufour speaks of the supper as 'a function of the relationship between Jesus and his disciples.'[41]

An action with bread and wine

This whole action is an action with bread and wine. These two elements are the medium that is here being set up between Jesus and his disciples. They are at the core of the whole action and become the focus of the reference to his death which Jesus is creating in this action of the last supper. Whatever is being established here is being established with bread and wine, which are presented to us in parallel: what is done with one is done with the other. This is clearer in the more developed style of the Marcan tradition than in the Antiochene. In the latter, the phrase 'in the same way' is used to indicate the actions with the cup, whereas in the former, there is the sign of liturgical development: the repetition of each action of Jesus with the cup in parallel to what he did with the bread.

Prophetic act

The accounts of the last supper are whole accounts consisting of actions and words. The words are part of the action and therefore need to be interpreted in conjunction with it.

The last supper is seen by exegetes as a prophetic action.[42] This is an important idea which forms the biblical basis for the link between the last supper and the cross. The prophets of the Old Testament often acted their prophecy.[43] This was not a mere matter of audio-visual acts but of the event beginning to happen because these actions came from the prophet who had insight into the counsels and plans of God. These actions came from the prophets (the seers) as truly as did their words. Once this action from God was done, it was done. One exegete describes the nature of the prophetic act in this way:

> A prophetic action is the realistic release of the energy of God, it is the irreversible setting in motion of his activity. It is as though I kicked a football towards a window: nothing can avert the catastrophe: I might just as well say that the window is already broken. And I still do have to wait for the actual crash of broken glass, the factual event that my careless boot has made inevitable. So it is with the prophetic act: it releases an event in miniature, it says that a particular consequence is not only possible, not simply predictable, it is unavoidable because it is already in being. Thus a prophetic act is not a prediction, it is the release of an inevitable circumstance which nothing can avert....[44]

The New Testament writers see the life of Jesus within this tradition. His whole life is seen as a sign from God: he is indeed the one who was to come, the anointed of God, who surpasses the prophets as one who effects God's plan. The supreme moment of this life is his death and resurrection. The last supper becomes crucial because in it, as a prophetic sign on the night before he died, he began his death and made the meaning of that death explicit. In that same sign done in his memory after his death, his disciples recognise him present among them beyond the power of death. They, of course, see this supper on the night before he died, in the light of their later experience which transforms its meaning for them. So this prophetic act of Jesus on the night before he died is already charged with a power which will manifest itself in the event of the next day and also in the event of the disciples' discovery of his presence when they do this action in his memory.

This is parallel to the meal eaten by the Israelites before their departure from Egypt. In the eating of the lamb whose blood had saved them, they had prophetically already left Egypt, the place of slavery and death.

The supper: word and action

Let us look now at the details of the event on the night before Jesus died as they are given to us in the narratives. The words accompanying the action with bread need to be seen in the context of that action: the bread is taken up by Jesus, God is blessed over it, it is broken and given to the disciples (each of these gestures has significance as we have seen). This taken, blessed, broken, given bread is handed to the disciples to be eaten with the words 'This is my body which will be given for you' (Luke) ... 'which is for you' (Paul) or 'Take it, this is my body' (Mark) or 'Take it, and eat,...' (Matthew). This was the bread which up to this time, they participated in as a sharing in God's blessing of creation, or as a sharing in the covenant relationship based on the exodus. They are now being given this bread as a sharing in the death of Jesus which was to happen the next day and therefore in the blessing which was going to accrue from that. They are given this bread in which they have God's blessing, and which is broken that many may become one from the same source of life. This bread is now identified with his body given over in death as the source of God's blessing and the unique source of life which draws all into communion. Whatever is true of bread, whatever is true of the exodus, has now reached its full truth in the death of Jesus.

The words accompanying the action with the cup also need to be seen in their relationship to the actions. The cup is taken, God is given thanks and praise over it and it is given to the disciples: 'This cup is the new covenant in my blood (Paul, Luke), 'which will be poured out for you' (Luke), or 'This is my blood, the blood of the new covenant, which will be poured out for many' (Mark, Matthew), 'for the forgiveness of sins' (Matthew).

This cup which they had been used to drinking as the joy-giving fruit of the vine, as witness of the fruitfulness and abundance of the earth, in memory of the exodus covenant and as a promise of *shalom* to come, they are now given to drink in memory of his blood poured out in death which will be the source of the blessings of salvation. They will take up this cup, the cup of life, the cup of salvation, the cup of fate as a participation in his death which will bring blessing upon them anew and definitively. Within these two sets of words over bread and cup there are some further important points to make for our understanding of the Eucharist.

The narratives do not present us with a body/blood pair as two separated parts of a human being. Exegetes are agreed that there is no such pairing off in the bible.[45] So we are not dealing with a presentation of bread equals body and wine equals blood separated from each other in the Eucharist. This has always been clear in the doctrine of the Church (Christ is present whole and entire under each species), but it is not always clear in the imagery we use and in popular devotion. In the Eucharist 'body' and 'blood' are used metonymically, that is, as 'part for the whole'. So 'body' is the whole person from a certain point of view; 'blood' is the whole person from a certain point of view. This is the same type of speech or writing that we engage in when someone says 'Martha has a heart of gold', which is a comment about Martha rather than her heart. Each of these words 'body', 'blood' have their own perspective to offer us on the death of Jesus.

Body

Body in the scriptures is used to indicate the person as experienced, as involved in relationships.[46] This usage is like the rather odd English use of 'body' as referring to oneself, e.g., 'how can a body be expected to put up with this?' In this phrase 'body' – means the person himself or herself. So when Jesus uses the word 'body' in the institution narratives he is referring to himself according to the usage of his time. There may be subtle overtones to the particular Aramaic word he used, overtones of fragility in the word similar to those expressed in the word 'flesh' (*sarx*) in the sixth chapter of John's Gospel.[47]

The phrase 'which will be given for you' (Luke) or 'which is for you' (Paul) in the Antiochene tradition are important because they link us into the servant of God tradition from the book of Isaiah. The servant's suffering is for others: 'Yet ours were the sufferings he was bearing, ours the sorrows he was carrying... he was being wounded for our rebellions, crushed because of our guilt, the punishment reconciling us fell on him' (Isa 53:4). The evocation of this biblical figure who was given by God to the people (Isa 42:1-9; 49:1-7) as one who would bring them back to God, sheds light upon the death of Jesus as an act of self-giving for us. So an interaction is set up between Jesus and this biblical tradition as a means of rendering meaning to Jesus' death.

Blood

In the scriptures 'blood' is about life. More accurately, it is about the life-principle. Blood is the place of life in us; it is where life is located. Blood is therefore sacred and untouchable because it belongs to God.[48] Israel was allowed to use blood for one purpose only and that was as a way of communicating with God to whom the blood/life belongs. And that had to be done properly. There were prescribed ways of making contact with the altar with it.[49] Blood was particularly associated with the covenant, with communion with God, and therefore with the expiation of sin. To speak of the 'blood' of Jesus, therefore, was to use a code taken from Jewish life and worship, a code which speaks of the pouring out of his life for us, of the giving over of Jesus' life-principle, which becomes our life-principle. This is captured in the beautiful double meaning of John's Gospel where Jesus renders up his spirit. (Jn 19:30) In this the new covenant in his blood is formed.

We have two different forms of the words of Jesus over the cup in the institution narratives. The Antiochene tradition has 'This cup is the new covenant in my blood which will be poured out for you' (Luke) and 'This cup is the new covenant in my blood' (Paul). The emphasis here, the point of focus, is the new covenant promised by the prophets Jeremiah (31:31-34) and Ezekiel (36:26-38). The old covenant of the exodus is in the background of the allusion but not in the foreground. The new covenant is formed in the death of Jesus as one who gives himself over for us. In Luke's version, we have a reference to the servant figure again: Jesus' blood 'poured out for you'.

In the Marcan tradition we have a formula whose primary allusion is to the making of the old covenant of the exodus which was in the blood of animals. The new covenant is, by contrast, in the blood of Jesus. Mark's Gospel says 'This is my blood, the blood of the covenant, which is to be poured out for many' and Matthew's Gospel adds 'for the forgiveness of sins'. If we read the account of the making of the old covenant, we will see the parallelism:

> Moses then took half the blood and put it into basins, and the other half he sprinkled on the altar. Then, taking the book of the covenant, he read it to the listening people, who then said, 'We shall do everything that Yahweh has said; we shall obey.' Moses then took the blood and sprinkled it over the people saying 'This is the blood of the covenant which Yahweh has made with you.' (Ex 24:6-8)

The focus here is on the blood of Jesus as that in which covenant is made (that is, his life poured out on the cross) over against the blood of animals in which the old covenant was made.

This blood is poured out for 'many'. There is a reference to the servant figure again in this phrase (Isa 53:11-12). 'The many' is a biblical term which indicates not 'many' as distinct from 'all', but 'the many' as the multitude, the whole crowd, which is humanity.[50]

We need to emphasise again that in speaking of blood poured out, we are always speaking of life poured out, life given. This has its basis in the very significance of blood.

Matthew's version adds 'for the forgiveness of sins'. This makes explicit a dimension of the death of Jesus contained already in the covenant: we are drinking into ourselves a relationship with God which involves communion with God which in turn involves the forgiveness of our sins.

Cup

The cup is prominent in these words. It is the wine in the cup, or the cup of wine that is being aligned with the blood/life of Jesus being poured out. We share in that by drinking this cup identified with that life given for us. We enter the new covenant, not by having blood sprinkled over us, but by sharing this cup of wine now identified with the blessing flowing from the death of Jesus.

In both the action over the bread and the action over the cup of wine, there is a presumption which carries over from the Old Testament. Just as it was presumed in Israel that by sharing bread, one could share the further blessings of God, for example, those given in the exodus, so it is presumed in these narratives that the primordial sign of God's blessing – bread – could bear other blessings with it, specifically those flowing from the death of Jesus. It is the same for the cup of wine.[51]

Leon-Dufour makes the important point that the Eucharist is presented in the New Testament as a part of the mystery of Jesus.[52] It is his action, his means of communication, not a mystery in its own right.

'The body of Christ'. 'The blood of Christ'. These words are said to us as we go to communion at Mass. The words come from the last supper narratives where they refer – each in their own way – to the death of Jesus on the cross the next day. This death of Jesus is his passover into the life of the resurrection. As we go to receive that communion in his body and blood, we receive communion in his passover, we go to receive communion in him who invites us to allow the pattern of his death and resurrection to be repeated in our lives.

Our doing what Jesus did:
the internal workings of the Eucharistic process

What we do in memory of Jesus is a ritual process which has a specific pattern. We engage in specific actions as we celebrate the Eucharist in his memory. These actions draw together what Jesus did and what we are doing. This explains the structure of the Eucharist and much of eucharistic theology.

We take up what he left us, by taking into our hands bread and wine which come from our kitchens! This is not normally true of the bread and wine we use in the Mass which have become stylised over the centuries; but bread and wine as such are among those human realities which belong in the kitchen and on the dining table. It is from these things that we take what we need for the Eucharist. Bread and wine follow a natural alimentary course. They are to be eaten, to be taken into us, to become part of the physical constitution of our bodies, and (as symbolic of all food) to assure our futures.

In the Eucharist, we take some of this bread and wine, that is, we take what should enter our bodies to assure the continuance of our lives, and we give it over to be taken up into the process of the Eucharist. To understand the Eucharist, we cannot afford to forget the origin of this bread and wine and the natural course into our bodies that they would normally have taken. We need to understand this to understand the eucharistic process. This leads us to see that in presenting bread and wine, which by its nature would have become part of us, we are presenting ourselves. It is thus that bread and wine represent and symbolise us, as we enter into a new direction through the process of the Eucharist.

In the Eucharist we take bread and wine and we recognise in them – in line with the biblical tradition elaborated earlier – the life-giving activity (the blessing) of God. Bread and wine – and particularly bread – speak to us of that incapacity to maintain our own life, our recognition that we receive our lives from beyond ourselves.

The bread and wine are presented before God in the presentation of the gifts as a recognition that all we are and have come from God. As we present to God what God has given us we do so in radical thanksgiving because that is all we can do before the living and life-giving God. The thanksgiving is the form in which we return ourselves to the one from whom we have come. The act of offering ourselves to God is enveloped in this thanksgiving. This describes the action of God's people in the first part of the eucharistic liturgy – the presentation of the gifts.

In the Eucharistic Prayer this action of the people of God is drawn into the action of praise and thanksgiving which Christ did on the night before he died.

We truly do what he did! On the night before he died Jesus took bread (and took the cup), and then blessed God (or gave God thanks and praise). That is, his own Jewish tradition put into his hands a ritual action and into his mouth a form of prayer which recognised God as God and giver of life and which, in that very fact, was a means by which Christ expressed his returning himself to the Father and the significance of his death the next day. He handed himself over to the Father, the

God of life, in the face of death; he returned himself to the Father even in the face of death. He trusted the God of life with his death. So the ritual meal of the passover became the means by which he indicated the meaning of his death. The two are drawn together.

In the Eucharist we do what he did in action and in prayer and in all that that prayed action means. The gathered community of the Church links with what he did as through, with, and in him it does now what he did on the night before he died and what he did on the cross.

As the bread and wine of the Jewish passover was not just a participation in the basic blessing of life given through all food, but in that blessing of life with God issuing from the exodus covenant, so the bread and wine of the Eucharist give us communion of life with God as that has come about in the death and resurrection of Jesus. We receive that communion of life, and at the same time, we are impelled by it to live out that communion with Jesus 'by doing what he did' in every sense of those words.

It is this eucharistic process and flow, which account for the need for the people of God to receive communion from that bread and wine which have been used in that action – in which they have recognised their utter dependence on God and have handed themselves over to God.

The Eucharist is the action of the community of the Church led by the priest, not the action of the priest attended and supported by the people. The spirituality of the Mass – our praying the Mass – falls back upon this process traced by the very actions and words of the eucharistic liturgy.

Sunday Eucharist

On the basis of what we have seen above, let us look at Sunday Eucharist. Because Sunday is the day on which the people of God are called together there is a qualitative difference between Sunday Eucharist and Eucharist on any other day of the week. The latter is a valuable form of devotion possible to only some among the people of God.

Sunday is the day when the assembling of God's people occurs in order that they may assert by that very gathering, by listening to the Word of God, by being drawn into eucharistic communion with the Lord and by being sent forth again that they are made Church. From what we have seen in the last few chapters the Sunday Eucharist is a full embodiment of the Eucharist precisely because the community is called together, making it the day of the covenant. A person absent from weekday Mass is no less a member of the Church, which finds its supreme manifestation in Eucharist, but if one does not gather with the community on a Sunday one is less a member of the covenant community. The Eucharist which is, of its very nature, the gathering of all into one, finds more authentic form in those eucharistic celebrations to which all are called.

The Eucharist establishes the Church, and in the memorial of Christ, it encounters again that Christ who is its origin and in whom its identity is founded. Christ is proclaimed as the risen one but also as the one who raises up the Church as his living body.

The Church's original gathering was the Sunday one, and because its sense of unity was strong there was only one Eucharist each Sunday, in each place. This unity was the sign of God's in-gathering of dispersed humanity. We can quote two Fathers of the Church insisting on this strong sense of unity. Ignatius of Antioch says: 'Be careful to have only one Eucharist, for there is only the one flesh of our Saviour Jesus Christ and only the one chalice in his blood; there is only one altar as there is only one bishop with his presbytery and deacons'.[53] St Augustine insists similarly: 'if we are not separated from each other, we are in unity, but if we are in unity, what are two altars doing in the same city?'.[55]

This strong insistence on unity was not always possible to achieve by one Eucharist in one city. In Rome there was another way of symbolising the one Eucharist and that was by means of the rite of the *fermentum* mentioned in the previous chapter. There were many communities in Rome and as a sign of unity, a part of the Eucharist from the pope's Mass was sent to the other churches where the Eucharist was being celebrated, placed in the chalice at these other celebrations, as a sign that it was the same Eucharist, the same mystery of unity being celebrated by the pope in the place where he was, as in all the other churches.[56]

This strong sense of unity came out of the Church Fathers' understanding of the link between the Eucharist and the Church. Even though different practices have arisen in the intervening centuries, we need to repossess this ancient stage of tradition as part of the renewal of our understanding of the Eucharist. Of its very nature, Sunday Eucharist differs qualitatively from Eucharist celebrated on other occasions.

Justice and peace at the table

In chapters ten and eleven of the first letter to the Corinthians, we see Paul shocked by the behaviour of his Corinthian Christians at the Lord's supper. They are split into factions, and while those who bring plenty of food, eat well, those who bring little, eat poorly or go hungry, and some begin to eat before all are ready. Paul's picture of the Corinthian Church and his complaints about it belong to those early years of the Church's life before the ritual actions of the Eucharist were separated from an actual meal. For Paul the Lord's supper was both eucharistic and physical nourishment, and he sees a contradiction between the way they are behaving at the Lord's supper and what that supper means. Their distinctions between rich and poor, their factionalism contradict this action by which they proclaim the future kingdom of God until God comes. They are not doing what Christ did; their actions do not open up space for God's coming.

In view of this attitude of Paul to the Eucharist, we need to ask questions about the fidelity of our own practice to the memory of the Lord. We need to ask: who are excluded from our table and why? Who are left aside in our celebrations of unity in Christ? People of nationalities other than the dominant nationality can be left aside or treated as second class. There are many 'little ones' whose sense of self is such that it is hard for them to approach the community. Hospitality is a reaching out of the community to those people who can be disregarded, as Christ was. To welcome them is to open up space to God's coming.

Whatever we do at Eucharist ought to be eucharistic! This is true of our use of money and our goods – are they for 'the many' as was the Christ who gathers us around him? Our collections need to be expressions of communion, the work of the whole Church supported in this spirit of communion. Our use of our money and resources is for the life of the world and of the Church. Not only was bread brought for Eucharist from people's kitchens in the early Church but for the poor and for the support of the Church and its ministers. What is to enter our bodies is given over to give life to the poor and to the Church as well as being taken up into the Eucharistic process.

Reflection

1. The symbolism of meal opens a door for us to understand the Eucharist. In what ways is it helpful?

2. How is the Sunday Eucharist a crucial dimension of being Christian?

3. Look into the meaning of the words and images in the institution narratives. How can they be a means of appreciating the Eucharist?

5 | 'He blessed . . . he gave thanks'

In the previous two chapters we have been looking at the Eucharist as doing what Jesus did. We now focus on one element of that action, the word dimension (the Eucharistic Prayer). In our symbolic action this corresponds to Jesus' action of blessing or giving thanks and praise to the Father: he blessed God over the bread, he gave thanks and praise over the cup. The prayer part of the action gives expression to the meaning of the whole, specifying the particular use of the meal symbol.

Let us now take a brief look at the development of the Eucharistic Prayer in the first four centuries of the Church's life and then present a theology of the Eucharistic Prayer.

The development of the Eucharistic Prayer

1. The eucharistic liturgy

In this section we look firstly at the development of the whole liturgy of the Eucharist. This is the context in which many of the specific developments of the Eucharistic Prayer have occurred. We look at deveopments in the naming of this action by Christians. The changes in the names given to the Eucharist indicate a larger development involving the changing shape of the action and the community's changing experience and understanding of the action.

In the earliest texts, what we call the Eucharist is referred to as 'the breaking of the bread' or 'the Lord's Supper'.[56] These two phrases indicate what the first Christians experienced when they gathered to fulfil Christ's command, and are an accurate description of this action. They experienced the specific actions and words done in memory of Jesus as part of a ritual meal, the Jewish ritual meal with a new point of reference in the death and resurrection of Jesus.

There were discernible developments within this form. In the institution narrative texts in the New Testament, Luke and Paul speak of the action of Jesus over the cup as being 'after the supper'. This phrase disappears in Mark and Matthew who simply have the two blessings in parallel. Scholars suggest that in Mark and Matthew we see the two specific memorial actions being drawn together rather than being separated by a meal.[57] It is suggested that the two blessings occurred before or after the actual meal, which at first would have continued to carry its own specific meal blessings as well.

Further development happened because we get the one blessing prayer over the bread and wine together, rather than the original form of two prayers. The longer blessing over the cup came to dominate in this merger. Eventually a complete separation occurred between the blessings in memory of Christ with their accompanying communion in the food over which they were prayed and the rest of the ritual meal which continued to be used as a meal of Christian fellowship and love – an *agape* meal.[58]

This action in memory of Jesus was eventually joined to the liturgy of the Lord whose origin lies in the synagogue. This shape is seen clearly by the middle of the second century in the writings of Justin Martyr.[59] Justin's description of the Christian assembly bears a striking similarity to our own experience of a Sunday liturgy.

In the midst of this development a new word for this action of the Church arose: *eucharistia*. (I will use the Latin word to distinguish this specific historical shape of the Eucharist from the continuing reference to the Christian memorial action as Eucharist).

Once the meal and the Christian memorial blessings were separated, people's experience of this action changed and their understanding of it took inevitable turns in accord with these changes. *Eucharistia* refers to the blessing prayer which is prayed over the bread and wine, and became a very prominent part of the community's experience of their gathering to remember Christ, as it moved into the forefront of people's attention. In the period between 100 and the early 200s a great deal seems to have happened in the development of these prayers, as we can see from the end result, though information on the actual process of the development is scanty.

In Greek (which was used as the common language throughout the Roman world) the word *eucharistia* was used to describe the whole action of the memorial meal. This name was taken from the prayer – the *eucharistia* (thanksgiving) – but the name was also applied to the bread and wine over which the prayer was prayed. We find terminology like to 'eucharistise the bread', 'bread eucharistised', 'bread of the Eucharist','the bread which becomes Eucharist'.[60]

We have Hippolytus saying that 'the offering be presented by the deacons to the bishop and that he eucharistise the bread into the antitypes of the body of Christ, the cup of wine into the image of his blood poured out'.[61]

To pray the *eucharistia* is to proclaim this prayer of thanksgiving over bread and wine, which foods become the bearers of the blessings for which God is thanked.

During the second and third centuries, there is a recurrent theme among Christian writers provoked by controversy with both Jews and pagans: the theme concerns the nature of Christian acts of worship. Unlike pagans and Jews Christians did not have identifiable sacrifices. Many pagans considered them atheists for this reason. The Fathers responded to this by saying that what they did in their praise and thanksgiving was a sacrifice in the form of prayer.[62] This brought the words 'offering' and 'sacrifice' on to the agenda and by the late third century we find these words being used to describe the Christian activity of the *eucharistia*.[63] Where *eucharistia* had been the enveloping notion which held within it the idea of offering, now the idea of offering becomes the enveloping notion which describes the nature of the thanksgiving. The very word used in the Eastern Churches to describe the Eucharistic Prayer was *anaphora* which means the offering. This was part of a development in which the forms of religiousness of the people of that time were finding genuine expression in Christianity, which was also seeking to mark out its difference: it had different sacrifices! This terminology will increase during the fourth century where the Church's Eucharist is shaped increasingly by its surrounding cultural forms and gradually becomes the public worship of the whole of society.

2. The Eucharistic Prayer

Throughout the middle ages, little was known about the Eucharistic Prayer. The moment of consecration had come to be considered paramount, the prayers surrounding it as secondary in importance. Awareness was lost of the fact that it was one prayer; several medieval commentators, following Isidore of Seville (d 631) described it as a series of prayers.

Commentators discussed where the Canon began and where it ended, some including the prayer over the gifts in its beginning, some the Lord's Prayer as its final part. Others excluded the Preface from its integral form.[64]

During the nineteenth century and into the twentieth century there was much theological discussion about the influence of ancient (Greek) mystery religions upon the development of the Christian liturgy. This included some discussion about the provenance of Eucharistic Prayers from such origins.

There well may have been some influence from these religions and the cultures to which they belonged on the development of Christian liturgies. However, the research and thoughtful study of the last thirty to forty years have brought to light the thoroughly Jewish and biblical origins of the Christian Eucharistic Prayers.

This was brought to the fore through a paper given by J.P.Audet called 'Literary Forms and Contents of a Normal Eucharistia in the First Century'.[65] Audet's thesis was that the origins of the Eucharistic Prayer were in Jewish and biblical blessing prayers – *berakah*. He presented a reconstruction of the literary form of a *berekah*: a blessing of God, followed by a statement of the motives for which we bless God. He postulated long blessings and short spontaneous blessings as the two forms of this genre. He regarded the two words, appearing in the institution narratives, 'blessed' (*eulogein*) and 'gave thanks and praise' (*eucharistein*) as equivalent in meaning; he saw both as references to the literary form of blessing as he postulated it.

As research and study went on, scholars were unhappy about two aspects of Audet's thesis. Firstly, they could not clearly identify this literary form as Audet reconstructed it and secondly, they were not happy with his equivalence of 'blessing' and 'giving thanks and praise'.

An important step was taken when Louis Ligier suggested that it was not a general literary form that was at the origin of the Eucharistic Prayer but a specific blessing prayer, which was the blessing over the cup at the end of the ritual meal, the *Birkat Hammazon*.[66] A similar thesis was put forward by Louis Bouyer in his book *Eucharist: Theology and Spirituality of the Eucharistic Prayer*.[67] This proposal gave a more concrete origin to the Eucharistic Prayer since the *Birkat Hammazon* was a text available in something like its first century form in the reconstruction made by Louis Finkelstein,[68] a Jewish scholar. Here is the text of this prayer as given by Finkelstein:

1. Blessed are you Lord our God, king of the universe, for you
2. nourish us and the whole world with goodness, grace
3. kindness and mercy.
4. Blessed are you, Lord, for you nourish the universe.
5. We will give thanks to you, Lord our God, because

you have
6. given us for our inheritance a desirable land, good and
7. wide, the covenant and the law, life and food. *(On feasts of Hanukkah and Purim, here follows an embolism[69].)*
8. And for all these things we give you thanks and bless your
9. name for ever and beyond.
10. Blessed are you, Lord our God, for the earth and for food.
11. Have mercy, Lord our God, on us your people Israel, and
12. your city Jerusalem, on your sanctuary and your
13. dwelling-place, on Zion, the habitation of your
14. glory, and the great and holy house over which
15. your name is invoked. Restore the Kingdom of the
16. house of David to its place in our days, and speedily
17. build Jerusalem
(on the feast of Passover, here follows an embolism[69])
18. Blessed are you, Lord, for you build Jerusalem. Amen.[69]

If we look at this text over against the texts of very early Christian Eucharistic Prayers given us in the *Didache* we can see some striking similarities.[70]

1. We give thanks to you, holy Father, for your holy name which
2. you have enshrined in our hearts, and for the knowledge
3. and faith and immortality which you made known to us
4. through your child Jesus
5. glory to you for evermore
6. You, Lord Almighty, created all things for the sake of your name
7. and gave food and drink to men for their enjoyment, that
8. they might give you thanks, but to us you have granted
9. spiritual food and drink for eternal life through
10. your child Jesus.
11. Above all, we give you thanks because you are mighty
12. glory to you for ever more. Amen.
13. Remember your Church, Lord, to deliver it from all evil and to
14. perfect it in your love, and bring it together from the four
15. winds, now sanctified, into your kingdom which you have

16. prepared for it, for yours are the power and the glory for ever more

17. Amen.

Thus we have above two prayers with very similar structures. We have a three-strophe structure: *Birket Hammazon* lines 1-4, 5-10, 11-18; *Didache* lines 1-5, 6-12, 13-17. Each of these ends with a final phrase blessing God, called a *chatimah*: *Birkat Hammazon*, lines 4, 10, 18; *Didache*, lines 5, 12, 16. Strophe one and two in the *Birkat Hammazon* are a blessing of God for the creation of a nourishing universe and it thanks God for what God has done in Israel's history. The first two strophes in the *Didache* prayer are about what God has done for God's people in Christ and then thanks God for nourishing creation. The order is reversed and thanksgiving has taken over from blessing as the leading prayer attitude.

In the third strophe in each prayer there is intercession for God's future activity, in the one case for God's people Israel, in the other for the Church.

Detailed scholarship seeking to isolate the earliest levels of tradition in Eucharistic Prayers, (work parallel to that done by biblical scholars on the gospel texts), has unearthed in both later texts and in fragments of earlier texts, an early level of tradition which shows us this 'strophic structure.[71]

It is increasingly clear that the development of the Eucharistic Prayer happened differently in different parts of the Church. It happened through the Church's presence in different cultures, through contacts between different areas of the Church, and through theological development. This diversified development carried on into the formation of the classical anaphoras of the fourth century which have family likenesses according to the part of the Church in which they arose; there are also differences within this general likeness.

Another important line of development in the study of the origins of the Eucharistic Prayer comes from the work of Cesare Giraudo in his two books *La Forma Litteraria della Preghiera Eucharistica* and *L'Eucharistia per le Chiesa*.[72] Giraudo works on the literary form of the *berakah* as he finds it in the scriptures and sees a strong continuity between it and the Eucharistic Prayers.

Giraudo also considers the *todah* (Hebrew root *YDH*) tradition of prayer in Israel to be crucial to an understanding of the Eucharist, and sees its specific origin in the confession of sin before God. *Todah* means to confess in the double sense of the word: to confess one's sin and infidelity before the God of the covenant while confessing God's goodness, God's greatness and God's absolute fidelity. This is the specific origin of the *todah*, but Giraudo sees the literary form as developing in less specific situations as a praise and thanksgiving to God for God's goodness, as acknowledgment of God's goodness. These prayers, he says, are standardised by the rabbis as *berakah* and by Christians as *eucharistia*, as thanksgiving. This preference for *eucharistia* may have been strengthened among Christians simply in opposition to rabbinical standardisation in terms of blessing. The New Testament usage of both probably represents a period of fluidity.[73]

According to Giraudo, these *todah* prayers have a patterned structure to them consisting of two parts: a recounting of the past followed by intercession that God act again now as in the past. He gives as an example Nehemiah 9:6-37, where all that God had done in the past is recounted (6-31), then after the phrase 'and now' or 'now therefore', the prayer continues asking God 'to count as no small thing their present misery...' (32-39), the phrase 'and 'now' or 'now therefore' being the pivot point of the two parts.[74]

He also quotes Nehemiah 1:5-11, to illustrate a developed example of this prayer, where the turning point is a quotation of God's word, recalling that word to God's mind as something God needs to act upon now. Thus, the scriptural passage is quoted in the liturgy as the grounding for what is about to be asked. Giraudo says that this is a regular scriptural usage quoting as evidence: Baruch 1-3; Esdras 9:6-15; 2 Samuel 7:18-29; 1 Kings 8:23-53; Exodus 32:11-13; 33:12-13; Numbers 14:13-19; Tobit 8; Judith 9:2-14; 2 Maccabees 6:12-15.[75] He also suggests that there are other prayers where a scripture passage is not quoted but is alluded to. Where the full quote is given, he calls it an embolism, where there is an allusion or a liturgical reworking of a scripture passage, he calls it a quasi-embolism.[76]

Giraudo suggests that this form of prayer is the basis of our Eucharistic Prayer. It recounts in a prayer of thanksgiving what God has done; then follows intercession that God act again. The embolism is the institution narrative, so there could be forms like Nehemiah 9:6-37 where there is no explicit embolism, forms where there is a formal embolism and forms where there is a quasi-embolism; so in some Eucharistic Prayers there could be no institution narrative, in others an institution narrative calling to God's mind why God should act now or yet in others simply an allusion to the institution narrative as a reason for God's acting now. This would explain why there is no institution narrative in some ancient prayers, why others could have an allusion to it and why others have complete institution narratives.[77]

The anaphora form became standard in the fourth and fifth century with all Eucharistic Prayers having an institution narrative. Many older prayers were probably given an institution narrative.

Once introduced, the institution narrative brings about changes in the form of the Eucharistic Prayer. It took time to draw the embolism in and as it was drawn in, it reshaped the prayer.[78] Giraudo's thesis is that the embolism came into the Eucharist in two different places: within the narrative, anamnetic or memorial section in some prayers and in the intercessory, epicletic section in others. This creates two basic categories of anaphora for him: anamnetic anaphoras and epicletic anaphoras.[79]

In the light of this background, Giraudo says that the *birkat hammazon* is not a three-strophied prayer as was suggested earlier. Rather, it has suffered from rabbinic standardisation in having the three final blessings (*chatimah*) added in to it. Without these he says we have the two parts: the thanksgiving narrative (*anamnesis*) and then the intercession that God act (*epiclesis*). Thus it fits his pattern. He goes on to seek his two-part pattern in all the prayers that our other authors would see as three-part.[80]

We have dealt with two approaches to the origin of the Eucharistic Prayer, because it shows the state of play in current research. We have a jigsaw puzzle in which the greater number of pieces is still missing! But some definite lines of development are emerging: the importance of Jewish prayer forms, attentiveness to differences in our texts, the fact that there was a reorganisation of Jewish life by the rabbis after the destruction of the temple and nation by the Romans. Because of the reorganisation, we cannot presume that what was happening after it, had been happening before. It is also important to present these different lines of development because each could represent what was going on in different parts of the Church. What Giraudo suggests would fit very well with the bipartite structure of the Eucharistic Prayer of Hippolytus where, following introductory rubrics (1 and 2), we find:

3. The Lord be with you:
   And all shall say:
   And with your spirit.
   Up with your hearts.
   We have them with the Lord.
   Let us give thanks to the Lord.
   It is fitting and right.
   And then he shall continue thus:

4. We render thanks to you, O God, through your beloved child Jesus Christ, whom in the last times you sent to us as saviour and redeemer and angel of your will;

5. who is your inseparable Word, through whom you made all things, and in whom you were well pleased.

6. You sent him from heaven into the Virgin's womb; and, conceived in the womb, he was made flesh and was manifested as your Son, being born of the Holy Spirit and the Virgin.

7. Fulfilling your will and gaining for you a holy people, he stretched out his hands when he should suffer, that he might release from suffering those who have believed in you.

8. And when he was betrayed to voluntary suffering that he might destroy death, and break the bonds of the devil, and tread down hell, and shine upon the righteous, and fix the limit, and manifest the resurrection,

9. he took bread and gave thanks to you, saying, 'Take, eat; this is my body, which shall be broken for you.' Likewise also the cup, saying, 'This is my blood, which is shed for you;

10. when you do this, you make my remembrance.'

11. Remembering therefore his death and resurrection, we offer to you the bread and the cup, giving you thanks because you have held us worthy to stand before you and minister to you.

12. And we ask that you would send your Holy Spirit upon the offering of your holy Church; that, gathering them into one, you would grant to all who partake of the holy things (to partake) for the fullness of the Holy Spirit for the confirmation of faith in truth,

13. that we may praise and glorify you through your child Jesus Christ, through whom be glory and honour to you, to the Father and the Son with the Holy Spirit, in your holy Church, both now and to the ages of ages. (Amen)[81]

We have thanksgiving narrative (*anamnesis*) ending in the account of what Jesus did on the night before he died with his command to us to repeat it in his memory. The prayer then obeys this command and prays that the Holy Spirit come. It pivots on the link 'therefore'.

Out of this period of development, of which we know little, there emerges in the fourth century the form that has come to be accepted as the classical form of this prayer, called the *anaphora* in the East, and eventually the *Canon Actionis* (The Form of the Action) in the West – what today we call the Eucharistic Prayer.

The characteristic of this form is the presence of the three elements: narrative of institution, *anamnesis* (memorial-offering) and *epiclesis* (calling upon the Spirit). These three elements lodge themselves into the Eucharistic Prayer and form it around themselves albeit in different ways. The Sanctus is also brought into the anaphora and settles other elements around itself: the introductory flow into it from the Preface, various kinds of links between it and the narrative-*anamnesis*-*epiclesis* (Roman Eucharistic Prayer III, IV). The intercession develops more detailed forms as time passes.

Older prayers are reshaped into this form often showing the seams where the pieces have been sewn together. These prayers arise in family patterns which are normally described as Antiochene, East Syrian, Alexandrian, Roman, Gallican and Mozarabic, corresponding to the different socio-cultural areas of the ancient Church. The tradition we have received in the Western Church is Roman with considerable influence from the Gallican rite which arose in Europe north of the Alps, and from the Mozarabic rite (the rite of Spain before the Roman Liturgy spread there). It is interesting that the ancient Roman Canon (Eucharistic Prayer I) is not really of the anaphoral form and is quite unique. These prayers were reaching standard forms at the same time as the crucial doctrines of Christology and Trinity were being defined in the Church.

The theology of the Eucharistic Prayer

To develop a theology of the Eucharistic Prayer, we need to go back to the two biblical words *berakah* (BRK) and *todah* (YDH) and look at the particular flavour that each of them has as a prayer form in Israel. These two have distinct backgrounds even though it is difficult at some periods of their history to distinguish them clearly. It is clear that the *todah* tradition gains great prominence in Christianity's development of its prayers. They all become emphatically eucharistic, and this word falls back upon the *todah* expressed in the use of the Greek *eucharistia* in our texts.

Berakah – blessing

The *berekah* is about the direct relationship between the person blessing God and God, expressed over a gift of God which is a blessing from God and which causes the person to bless God, to give expression to their relationship to God, and is essentially an expression of this relationship.

Blessing has strong links to God as the creating God who blessed human beings at the beginning with life and fruitfulness (Gen 1:22.28). This blessing is passed on and is recognised in children who are a blessing from God – they are the blessing which evidences the life and fruitfulness with which God has blessed humanity. God is blessed for them.

Food is a blessing over which our relationship with the blessing God is celebrated in prayer. Again this has to do with God as creator, as life-giver.

God's covenant is also presented as a blessing, as life-giving and fructifying; so the covenant with Noah (Gen 9:1), with Abraham (Gen 12:2; 17:1-22;) with Isaac (Gen 26:3). The Sinai covenant and the Torah are likewise a blessing (Deut 30:15-20). God's blessing is about life and propensity which we recognise and for which we bless God. All of life is referred to God in blessing.

Blessing invokes the reciprocal relationship between God and God's people. God is recognised as blessing them in life-giving activities and gifts for which they bless God. This is the reciprocal flow going on between God and God's people.

Todah – confession, acknowledgment

The other important word from Israel's prayer tradition is *todah*. Its range of meaning includes 'recognition, acknowledgment, confession, praise and thanks'.[82] The background to this prayer has a different flavour from that of *berakah* even though the words are clearly related. The root meaning of the word is 'to make known', so the word is related to proclamation in the sense used by Paul in 1 Corinthians 11:26 where he speaks of proclaiming the Lord's death. God is made known, is proclaimed in the *todah* – the confession, the proclamation of God's people. The background to this has to do with the particular discovery that God's self-revelation now, is the same as God's self-revelation in the great events of Israel's history. It is Israel's response to this rediscovery of the God of the exodus, who, in the present, is still delivering the people (or an individual among the people). It can also be a prayer which ends in trust that God will deliver again the people (or a faithful person) from present distress by God's self-revelation as the God of those events. This comes to the fore particularly in the psalms of lamentation.[83] Here God is recognised again, acknowledged, proclaimed, praised.

This is linked to 'gospel'. In this praise and thanksgiving, the gospel, the good news of God's fidelity is proclaimed, and is even contained within it. In this sense we see the meaning of Paul's use of the word 'proclaim' – the Lord's supper proclaims the good news of Jesus' death: God is recognised at work in it.

Leon-Dufour makes the point that these prayers were associated with communion sacrifices which were called thanksgiving sacrifices. The prayers could also replace these sacrifices as they did in the Diaspora where the material sacrifices were not possible. This makes these prayers 'sacrifices in the form of words', an important element in the movement towards recognising realities like prayer and almsgiving as sacrifices in themselves. This movement was afoot at the end of New Testament times.[84]

Jesus' use of these prayers

On the night before he died, it was prayers of these kinds – *berakah* and *todah* – that his own Jewish tradition put into the mouth of Jesus. It was not just certain formulae, whatever they may have happened to be, but a spirituality built up within and around them that was given to him on that night as had been the case on so many other occasions of his life as a practising Jew.

As he approaches his death which he has come to out of his relationship with his Father, he finds himself with these prayers with which to celebrate his relationship to his Father.

We may presume that he comes before the God of Israel at around passover time, and blesses this God for the blessings of food and covenant by which God has given and continues to give life. In Jesus the ancient faith of Israel in the God who blesses meets Jesus' own experience of his Father, of his mission, and of the death to which his mission has brought him.

We may presume also that he comes before the God of Israel before whom God's people come as the God of the exodus: the God who is expected to be revealed as the deliverer when they find themselves in distress. In Jesus these forms of the prayer of his people meet his own situation of distress and his sense of mission from the Father.

Do not these prayers within their tradition offer to Jesus the means of expressing his inner attitudes as he moves towards his death? Do they not offer him a means of expressing his returning of himself to the Father in blessing, an expression of trust in the Father upon whom he can rely in distress because the Father is the God who was revealed as the deliverer in the exodus? Does it not give him a natural means of referring to his death the next day as he sees it caught up in his mission from the Father; a natural means, given him within Israel's tradition, to interpret his death?

The Christian Eucharistic Prayer

The provenance of Christian Eucharistic Prayers has become clear, even though we cannot demonstrate how the development has occurred in all its phases. Their origin lies in the Jewish tradition of prayers, described as *berakah* and *todah* whose character we have just considered.

Thanksgiving became the standard Christian form of prayer over food in the action done in memory of Jesus. So we find Christians from very early on being invited into this prayer with a formula very like 'Let us give thanks to the Lord our God'.

However we describe the emergence of the Eucharistic Prayer out of the Jewish prayers, the two fundamental prayer attitudes which come through are praise/thanksgiving (or just thanksgiving) and supplication. This was true of the three-strophe prayers of the *birkat hammazon* and the *Didache* and of the line of development suggested by Giraudo – narrative thanksgiving followed by intercession, the like of which we saw also in the prayer of Hippolytus.

This pattern is present in our current Eucharistic Prayers. They begin in thanksgiving which gives them their very names and they always conclude in intercession. Between these two sections are several elements which we will consider in due course.

Another dimension is drawn out of these prayers of thanksgiving and supplication by that part of the prayer that lies between them: the narrative of institution, the *anamnesis* (memorial), and the *epiclesis*.

Thanksgiving and supplication are important because of their link to the central concept of eucharistic theology: memorial. Their placement and importance flow from all we saw in the chapter on memorial. They flow out of the link between the past event giving us our origin and the present moment.

The Church existing before God in the present moment depends totally for its existence and identity on what God did in Christ's death and resurrection. The Church has been raised to life in Christ's passover to the Father. This has happened to the Church as the first fruits of the harvest, the initial ingathering which already rejoices in what God is doing for the whole of humanity which in turn will rejoice in this gift when Christ comes again.

The Church exists in the present because God has acted in Christ in the past and has brought us to this moment. We live in Christ; we receive now the blessings which have been bestowed upon us in Christ we live this in faith now. What God did on the 'day' of Christ's death and resurrection, God is doing among us now. So the Eucharistic Prayer recounts this mystery of our present explained by our past.

The Church existing in the present 'out of the past event' stands before its own future and the future of humanity in a world that is simply not good enough: the way things are cannot continue to be! All the forces which brought about Christ's death are still active and destructive in our world and so there must be Christian dissatisfaction, expressed in the Christian call to Christ to come again! Our prayer is oriented to the future and we move into that future in the expectation that God will continue to do what was done in Christ. We move into every stage of human history within the present offered us by Christ's death and resurrection and seek to find God at work there.

The Eucharistic Prayer is radically historical prayer, and from this, thanksgiving and supplication arise naturally, based on the meaning of memorial.

Thanksgiving is a profound religious attitude in which we recognise that all we are and have come from God, that God has given us even to ourselves, that there is nothing we can give to God. All we can do is return to God what we have received, render ourselves up to God, which we do in thanksgiving. It is the form in which we return ourselves to God from whom we have come, and the circle of origin and return between God and human beings is completed in a profound and radical recognition that God is God.

This is taken up into our relationship with God in Christ, becoming the form in which we recognise the continuing working of God in Christ to bring us and all of humanity to God. We bring ourselves before God in thanksgiving in order that we might be further penetrated and possessed by that mystery which we have already received. In that further penetration and possession our world, as it is in us, is being redeemed.

Like thanksgiving, supplication is the natural approach to God out of memorial. We come before God asking that what God has begun may come to fulfilment for the completion of what was begun in Christ. Our own experience of incompleteness, pain and evil, and these things as we see them in our world, bring us before God who has overcome evil, who has brought us to God's very self. Intercession or supplication is not a later addition to the Eucharistic Prayer, but is original in their texts and the texts of their Jewish predecessors, arising out of the very character of these prayers as they themselves arose out of the nature of memorial.

Thanksgiving and intercession are the most original elements of the Eucharistic Prayer.

It was said earlier that the central part of the Eucharistic Prayer, which comes between the thanksgiving and the intercession, draws out the full meaning of this thanksgiving and supplication. The narrative of institution, the *anamnesis* and the *epiclesis* draw out the essence of this thanksgiving and intercession of this group of people who are doing now what Christ did, in the course of which action they enter into communion with the same Christ by means of the bread and wine over which this prayer is prayed. In that communion they become his body, the Church.

The institution narrative is the Church's warrant to do this action. The Church's action is grounded now in that act of Christ on the night before he died. In it the Church obeys the command given at the end of that act: 'do this in memory of me'.

In the *anamnesis* or memorial prayer which follows the institution narrative (after the memorial acclamation), the Church explicitly acknowledges what it is doing in this act, expressing its explicit self-consciousness of its eucharistic act. It is all expressed in the liturgical 'we', the gathered church which is the subject of this action. So we have: 'Father, we celebrate the memory of Christ, your Son. We, your people and your ministers recall his passion... and from the many gifts you have given us, we offer you...' (Eucharistic Prayer I); 'In memory of his death and resurrection, we offer you, Father...' (Eucharistic Prayer II); 'Father, calling to mind the death your Son... we offer you...' (Eucharistic Prayer III); 'Father, we now celebrate the memorial of our redemption. We recall Christ's death..., we offer you...' (Eucharistic Prayer IV).

This is the core moment of the Church's act, where the whole prayer is gathered into the Church's possession and our ownership of it is asserted. The Church here stands with Christ before the Father and hands itself over with Christ to be the raw material for the kingdom's coming as Christ did on the night before he died. We hand over ourselves, with our bread and wine, by means of which we become the bearers of the mystery which we will receive in Communion.

In the *epiclesis* we pray that the Spirit will come upon this action as the Spirit came upon the Church at Pentecost and bring about that communion between Christ and ourselves spoken of in the *anamnesis*. The *epiclesis* was originally a single element in the Eucharistic Prayer. It prayed that, by the power of the Spirit, the whole mystery of the passover be brought about in the whole eucharistic action. In the Eucharistic Prayers published since Vatican II, the *epiclesis* has been formulated in two parts: the first praying for the Spirit's transformation of the gifts before the institution narrative; the second praying for the transformation of the Church, placed after the *anamnesis*.

These three elements: institution narrative, *anamnesis* and *epiclesis* are dimensions of the whole eucharistic mystery rather than three successive parts of the progress of the Eucharistic Prayer. The action expressing our doing what Jesus did is the *anamnesis* and the narrative is the ground for this action. The narrative warrants us to do what Jesus did, and in this lies the real and reciprocal presence and action of Christ and his Church, brought about by the Spirit who initiated that communion between Christ and his Church at Pentecost.

These elements highlight that our thanksgiving and intercession are ours and Christ's united in that mystery of communion which is the Church. In each part of the Eucharistic Prayer a dimension of the mystery we are celebrating is drawn out and becomes, therefore, a unity of various movements which bring to the surface aspects of the mystery of communion between Christ and his Church.

This prayer expresses 'the offering of your Church'. It is upon this offering that the ancient prayer of Hippolytus asks God to send the Spirit. The Church comes before God in the action of offering this bread and wine and asking that God send the Spirit upon this action. The Church does this action in the state of remembering and thanksgiving (present participles): remembering Christ's death and resurrection and thanking him that it can stand before him and serve him. All of this is done in response to his command following the account of institution: do this in memory of me. This concept of the Eucharist is embedded in our earliest versions of the *Roman Canon*, the present first Roman Eucharistic Prayer. Here the *quam oblationem* (bless and approve our offering) prayed not that 'it becomes for us the body and blood of Jesus Christ...' but that it becomes 'the image and likeness of the body and blood of Christ'. The terminology falls back upon an earlier sacramental theology where our action is seen as the image and likeness or the type of Christ's action. This means that it captures in itself now that action of Christ as Old Testament types really had Christ and his action hidden within them.[85] So the Church does now what Christ did then, and prays that this action, as the true action of Christ, now done by the Church, will be accepted by God as an action done by Christ, just as the sacrifices of old were accepted by God, not on their own merits but because Christ's action was really anticipated in them.

'Lord, look upon this offering of your Church and accept it as once you accepted the gifts of your servant Abel, the sacrifice of Abraham our father in faith and the bread and wine offered by your priest Melchisedech.'

Eucharistic Prayer I prays that the sacrifice which is a figure (image and likeness) of Christ's sacrifice, after it occurred, will be accepted, just as these sacrifices of old were all accepted because they were types (images and likenesses) of Christ's sacrifice before it happened historically.

The prayer then prays:

Almighty God,
we pray that your angel may take this sacrifice
to your altar in heaven.
Then as we receive from this altar
the sacred body and blood of your Son,
let us be filled with every grace and blessing.

The transformation of the gifts is seen to occur through the taking of these gifts to God's altar rather than through the action of the Holy Spirit. We have very different imagery at work. This imagery was derived probably from a Jewish-Christian theology given the very Jewish character of the early Church in Rome.[86]

A good deal of work still needs to be done on the development of the formulae of the Eucharistic Prayers. Many formulations of the *anamnesis* are rather unclear.[87] The identification of the institution narrative as the moment of consecration and the mentality accompanying that view put the rest of the prayer into a secondary status and we lose the sense of movement innate in the prayer.

Our prayers naturally bear within them the marks of the cultures of their origins, which sometimes makes it hard to identify our real world in them. It is important that greater imaginative unity between these core prayers of the Church and contemporary Christians be established, since these prayers have to do with the expression, discovery and development of our identity and solidarity!

Reflections

1. Reflect and share your thoughts on one of the current Eucharistic Prayers.

2. If the Eucharistic Prayer gives expression to the core of the Christian faith, what would you say are the main characteristics of Christian prayer?

3. Reflect and share how you react to the statement: 'intercession as an expression of Christian dissatisfaction.'

Conclusion

In this book we have looked at the Eucharist as an action which we do in communion with Jesus, the risen Lord. There are two sources of the meaning of this action – the paschal mystery of Jesus and the action which we do in memory of that passover through death to a new risen human life in Christ. We 're-source' ourselves in this mystery of Christ and we live it out, called to embody it in our lives and history and to make it explicit and active in the human history of which we, the Church, are a part. The presence of Christ in this mystery calls us and enables us to be the priestly, prophetic and kingly people of God like Christ who lived out these characteristics in his person and mission. This is the beginning of a eucharistic theology!

Notes

Memorial

[1] X. Leon-Dufour, *Sharing the Eucharistic Bread*, Mahwah: Paulist Press, 1987, 174-5.

[2] Leon-Dufour, *op. cit.*, 102-16; Brevard S. Childs, *Memory and Tradition in Israel*, London: SCM, 1962, 31-65; C. Westermann, *Praise and Lament in the Psalms*, Atlanta: John Knox Press, 1981, 214-49.

[3] Childs, *op. cit.*, esp. 53-55.

[4] Leon-Dufour, *op. cit.*, 102-4; Childs, *op. cit.*, 31-65; J. Jeremias, *The Eucharistic Words of Jesus*, London: SCM, 1966, 237-55.

[5] Y. Congar, 'The Church and Pentecost', in *The Mystery of the Church*, London: Geoffrey Chapman, 1965, 148-9.

[6] *The Roman Missal*: Preface for Sundays in Ordinary Time VII.

[7] Thomas Aquinas, *Summa Theologiae*, III, Q. 60, art. 2.

[8] H. Dondaine, 'La Definition des sacrements dans la "Somme Theologique"', in *Revue des Sciences Philosiphique et Theoloqique* 31, 1947, 213-28; D. Burke, 'Introduction', *St Thomas Aquinas, Summa Theologiae*, London: Blackfriars, Eyre & Spottiswoode, 1975, Vol. 56, XIII-XXIII.

[9] Augustine, Sermon 272, PL 38, 1246-48.

[10] See H. De Lubac, *Corpus Mysticum*, Paris: Aubier, 1944, esp. 89-115; J. M. R. Tillard, *Chair de l'Eglise, Chair du Christ*, Paris: Cerf, 1992, 47-97; G. Békès, 'The Eucharist Makes the Church,' in R. Latourelle, ed., *Vatican II: Assessment and Perspectives*, New York: Paulist Press, 1989, 347-63; P. McPartlan, 'Eucharistic Ecclesiology' in *One in Christ*, Vol. XXII, 4, 1986, 314-331; J. Theisen, 'Images of the Church and the Eucharist,' in *Worship* 58, 3, 1984, 117-29.

[11] E. Schillebeeckx, *The Eucharist*, London: Sheed and Ward, 1968, 137ff.

[12] S. T. III, q. 66, art. 1; q. 72, art. 5, ad 3; q. 73, art, 1, ad 3.

[13] S. T. III, q. 60, art. 3.

[14] Childs, *op. cit.*, 70-73; Leon-Dufour, *op. cit.*, 224-227.

The last supper and the Eucharist

[15] X. Leon-Dufour, *op. cit.*, 306-8; J. Jeremias, *op. cit.*, 15-87; A Jaubert, *The Date of the Last Supper*, New York: Alba House, 1965.

[16] E. Mazza, *The Eucharistic Prayers of the Roman Rite*, New York: Pueblo Publishing Company, 1986, 28-9; U. Eco, *Semiotics and the Philosophy of Language*, Bloomington: Indiana University Press, 1986, 164-88.

[17] *In Proditione Judae*, Hom. 1, 6. PG 49, 380.

[18] V. Saxer, 'Figura Corporis et Sanguinis Domini. Une Formule Eucharistique des premiers siecles chez Tertullien, Hippolyte et Ambroise', in *Rivista di Archeologia Christiana* 47, 1971, 65-89; Idem, 'Terullian', in *The Eucharist of Early Christians*, New York: Pueblo Publishing Company, 1978, 132-55; E. Mazza, *Mystagogy*, New York: Pueblo Publishing Company, 1989, esp. 1-13.

[19] *The Roman Missal*, Third Eucharistic Prayer: 'Look with favour on your Church's offering, and see the victim whose death has reconciled us to yourself.'

[20] E. Mazza, *The Eucharistic Prayers*, 68-73.

[21] See E. Schillebeeckx, *The Church with a Human Face*, London: SCM, 1985, 42-73; R. Brown, *Priest and Bishop*, New York: Paulist Press, 1970; H-M Legrand, 'The Presidency of the Eucharist' in *Worship* 53, 5, 1979, 413-37; K. B. Osborne, *Priesthood. A History of the Ordained Ministry in the Roman Catholic Church*, New York: Paulist Press, 1988, esp. 41-83.

[22] P. Nautin, 'Le rite de "fermentum" dans les eglises urbaines de Rome,' *Ephemerides Liturgicae* 96, 1982, 510-22. N. N. De Boulet, 'Titres urbains et communautè dans la Rome Chrétiènne' in *La Maison Dieu* 36, 1953, 14-32.

[23] See, for example, Schillebeeckx, *op. cit.*, 141-47; A. Mirgeler, *Mutations of Western Christianity*, London: Burns and Oates, 1964, 92-120; R. Markus, *The End of Ancient Christianity*, Cambridge University Press, 1990, 220-28; D. N. Power, *Ministers of Christ and his Church*, London: Geoffrey Chapman, 1969, 30-126.

[24] P. Bradshaw, *Ordination Rites of the Ancient Churches of East and West*, New York: Pueblo Publishing Company, 1990, esp. 215-35; D. N. Power,

op. cit., 87-144.

25 In *II Corinthians*, Hom 18, 3. PG 61, 527.

26 F. Van der Meer, *Augustine the Bishop*, London: Sheed and Ward, 1983, 397-402.

A meal

27 W. Brueggeman, *Israel's Praise*, Philadelphia: Fortress Press, 1988, 30.

28 *General Instruction on the Roman Missal*, art. 48.

29 X. Leon-Dufour, *op. cit.*, 32-46; G. Feeley-Harnik, *The Lord's Table*, Philadelphia: University of Pennsylvania Press, 1981; I. H. Marshall, *Last Supper and Lord's Supper*, Exeter: The Paternoster Press, 1980, 13-29.

30 G. Giraudo, *Eucharistia per la Chiesa*, Roma: Gregorian University Press, 1989, 155ff; T. Talley, 'The Literary Structure of the Eucharistic Prayer', in *Worship* 58/5, 1984, 404-20.

31 J. Kodell, *The Eucharist in the New Testament*, Wilmington: Michael Glazier, 1988, 38-52; S. Cavaletti, 'The Jewish Roots of Christian Liturgy' in ed. E. S. Fisher, *The Jewish Roots of Christian Liturgy*, Mahwah: Paulist Press, 1990, 17-30.

32 G. S. Sloyan, 'Jewish Ritual of the First century C. E. and Christian Sacramental Behaviour', in *Biblical Theology Bulletin* 15/3 1985, 98-103; C. DiSante, *L'Eucharistia, Terra di Benedizione* Bologna: Edizioni Dehoniane, 1987.

33 Leon-Dufour, *op. cit.*, 32-54.

34 Mk 2:15-17; Mt 11-19; Lk 15-2; 19:1-10.

35 For example, 1 Cor 10-11; Jn 6; For the development of this theme, see F. J. Moloney, *A Body Broken for a Broken People*, Blackburn: Collins Dove, 1990, p20-8;39-49;55-64; J. Kodell, *op. cit.*,p84-8;94-6;106-113;118-129

36 Leon-Dufour, *op. cit.*, 157-81; P. Bradshaw, *A Search for the Origins of Christian Worship*, London: SPCK, 1992, 47-55.

37 Mk 14:17-24; Mt 26:20-28; Lk 22:14-20; 1 Cor 11:23-26.

38 Leon-Dufour, *op. cit.*, 82-95.

39 *Ibid*, 96-101.

40 Leon-Dufour, *op. cit.*, 102-56; J Delorme (et al), *Eucharist in the New Testament*, London: Chpaman 1964; E. Kilmartin, *The Eucharist in the Primitive Church*, Prentice Hall, Englewood Cliffs, NJ, 1965; Kodell, *op. cit.*; Moloney, *op. cit.*; I. H. Marshall, *op. cit.*

[41] Leon-Dufour, *op. cit.*, 61.

[42] J. W. Bowker, 'Prophetic Action and Sacramental Form' in *Texte und Untersuchungen*, Vol. 89, Studia Evangelica IV, 1964, 129-37. See also authors in note 40.

[43] Ezek 4-5; Jer 19:10ff, 28:10; Isa 20:1ff; 8:1ff; 1 Kings 22:11; 2 Kings 13:14-19.

[44] Bowker, *op. cit.*, 130.

[45] Leon-Dufour, *op. cit.*, 63-4.

[46] *Ibid*, 119-20; Giraudo, *op. cit.*, 204-14; J. A. T. Robinson, *The Body*, London: SCM, 1952.

[47] Leon-Dufour, *op. cit.*, 63-4.

[48] Leon-Dufour, *op. cit.*, 140-44; Giraudo, *op. cit.*, 231-36; R. Daly, *Christian Sacrifice*, Washington: Catholic University of America Press, 1978, 87-138.

[49] R. Daly, *op. cit.*, 117-34.

[50] Leon-Dufour, *op. cit.*, 173-4.

[51] G. Sloyan, *op. cit.* 99-100.

[52] Leon-Dufour, *op. cit.*, 60-1.

[53] Letter to the Philadelphians, 4. See J. Sparks (ed) *The Apostolic Fathers*, Nashville: Thomas Nelson, 1978, 105.

[54] *Ep. Johannis in Parthos.* Tract III, 7. PL35, 2001.

[55] N. N. DeBoulet, *op. cit.*, 14-32.

'He blessed ...he gave thanks'

[56] Acts 2:42, 46; 20:7; 20:11; 1 Cor 10:16; Didache 14:1; Ignatius of Antioch to the Ephesians 20.2. See Sparkes (ed), *op. cit.*, 83-4.

[57] Leon-Dufour, *op. cit.*, 157-81; L. Ligier, 'From the Last Supper to the Eucharist' in (ed) L. Sheppard, *The New Liturgy*, London: Darton, Longman and Todd, 1970, 113-50; Kilmartin, *op. cit.*

[58] A. Hamman, 'Quelle est L'origine del'agape? in *Texte und Untersuchungen*, Studia Patristica 10, 1970, Vol. 107, 351-354; P. Bradshaw, *The Search for the Origins of Christian Worship*, Chapter 4, passim.

[59] First Apology 67.1-8. See (eds) R. C. D. Jasper and G. J. Cuming, *Prayers of the Eucharist, Early and Reformed*, London: Collins, 1980, 19-20.

[60] Justin Martyr, First Apology 66.1. See Jasper and Cuming (eds), *op.*

cit., 19; Ignatius of Antioch, Smyr. 7.1; Phil. 4, see Sparkes (ed), 105, 112; Didache 9.5, see Jasper and Cuming (eds), 14-15; Irenaeus, Against the Heretics 18.5, see D. N. Power, *Irenaeus of Lyons on Baptism and Eucharist* Alcium/GRDW Liturgical Study 18, Bramcote, Notts, 1991, 21.

61 Apostolic Tradition, see G. J. Cuming (ed), *Hippolytus: A Text for Students*, Bramcote: Grove Books, 1976, 21.

62 Justin Martyr, Dialogue with Trypto 117, 3, see Jasper and Cuming (eds), *op. cit.*, 18.

63 See V. Saxer, 'Terullian' and R. Johanny, Cyprian of Carthage' in (ed.) W. Rodorf *The Eucharist of Early Christians*, New York: Pueblo Publishing Company, 1978, 132-155; 156-181.

64 J. A. Jungmann, *The Mass of the Roman Rite*, (one volume edition) Westminster: Christian Classics, 1978, 362-68.

65 Studia Evangelica, *Texte and Untersuchungen*, 73 (1959), 643-62.

66 L. Ligier, 'From the Last Supper to the Eucharist' in L. Sheppard (ed), *op. cit.*, 113-50.

67 Indiana: University of Notre Dame Press, 1968.

68 *Jewish Quarterly Review* 19, 1928, 211-62.

69 This text has been cut down from Finkelstein's version in which there follows a fourth blessing which is certainly of later origin (Ligier). The embolism for Passover is also left out here. An embolism is an expansion or an insertion which specifies the feast celebrated that day and its significance for Israel.

70 Didache 10:1-6, see Jasper and Cuming (eds), *op. cit.*, 15.

71 Ligier, 'From the Last Supper...'; H. Wegman, 'Genealogie hypothetique de la priere eucharistique' in *Questions Liturgiques* 61, 1980, 263-278.

72 *La Forma Litteraria...*, Rome: Biblical Institute Press, 1981, *L'Eucharistia...*, Rome: Gregorian University Press, 1989.

73 Giraudo, *Eucharistia...*, 199ff.

74 *Ibid*, 282ff.

75 *Ibid*, 293ff, 312ff.

76 Ibid, 349, 353.

77 *Ibid*, 325-7.

78 *Ibid*, 359-60.

79 *Ibid*, 352ff.

80 *Ibid*, 155-7.

81 R. C. D. Jasper and G. S. Cuming (eds), *op. cit.*, 22-3.

82 Giraudo, *Eucharistia*, 277ff; H. H. Guthrie, *Theology as Thanksgiving*, New York: Seabury Press, 1981; Leon-Dufour, *op. cit.*, 42-4.

83 Childs, *op. cit.*, 60-5; Brueggeman, *op. cit.*, 85-7, 129-47.

84 Leon-Dufour, *op. cit.*, 42-5; Guthrie, *op. cit.*, 145ff.

85 E. Mazza, *The Eucharistic Prayers*, 111-20; 168-83.

86 R. E. Brown and J. P. Meier, *Antioch and Rome*, New York: Paulist Press, 1983, 92-104.

87 See comments in the respective articles and chapters in L. Sheppard (ed), *op. cit.*, and E. Mazza, *op. cit.*

Bibliography

Eucharist in the scriptures

Leon-Dufour, X., *Sharing the Eucharistic Bread*, Mahwah: Paulist Press, 1987.

A thorough presentation of the Eucharist in the New Testament which outlines in detail the present state of scholarship on many key issues. It is a profound work but not complex. It merits careful reading for its theology and for the spiritual nourishment it offers.

Kodell, J., *The Eucharist in the New Testament*, Wilmington: Michael Glazier, 1988.

A short and very readable presentation. Quite adequate.

Moloney, F. J., *A Body Broken for a Broken People*, Melbourne: Collins Dove, 1990.

Considers the major eucharistic texts in the New Testament within the context of the whole New Testament, bringing out points of important pastoral interest and giving a greater sense of the feel for the Eucharist in each New Testament author.

Systematic Theology of the Eucharist

Power, D. N., *The Eucharistic Mystery: Revitalizing the Tradition*, New York: Crossroad, 1992.

The most striking presentation of a contemporary theology of the Eucharist that we have in the English language. Not always easy reading, but well worth the effort.

Moloney, R., *The Eucharist*, London: Geoffrey Chapman, 1995. An extremely useful and readable book dealing with the major topics of interest in eucharistic theology.

McPartlan, P., *The Eucharist Makes the Church*, Edinburgh: T & T Clark, 1993.

A presentation of the work of Henri de Lubac and John Zizioulas on the relationship between the church and the Eucharist, a major eucharistic theme in theology at present.

Reumann, J., *The Supper of the Lord*, Philadelphia: Fortress Press, 1985.

An excellent presentation of the treatment of the Eucharist in the New Testament and in current ecumenical dialogues. Very useful for both eucharistic theology and ecumenism.

Mazza, E., *The Eucharistic Prayers of the Roman Rite*, New York: Pueblo Publishing Company, 1986.
The best contemporary single volume presentation of the current Eucharistic Prayers.

Further reading

Békès, G., 'The Eucharist Makes the Church'. In R. Latourelle (ed.) *Vatican II: Assessment and Perspectives*, Mahwah: Paulist Press, 1989, 347-63.

Bowker, J.W., Prophetic Action and Sacramental Form. Texte und Untersuchgungen Vol. 89, *Studia Evangelica* IV (1964), p. 129-137.

Bradshaw, P.F., *Ordination Rites of the Ancient Churches of East and West* NY: Pueblo Publ Co, 1990.

Brandts, A., 'Church and Sacrament'. *Questiones Liturgiques* 75, 1994, 1/2, 56-69.

Brown, R.E., *Priest and Bishop*. London: Geoffrey Chapman, 1971.

Brown, R.E., Meier, J.P., *Antioch and Rome*. NY, Ramsey: Paulist Press, 1983.

Cavaletti, S., The Jewish Roots of Christian Liturgy, in ed. E.S. Fisher, *The Jewish Roots of Christian Liturgy*, Mahwah: Paulist Press, 1990. 17-30

Chauvet, L. M., 'What Makes the Liturgy Biblical? – the Actions'. *Studia Liturgica* 22, 1992, 2, 121-33.

Childs, B., *Memory and Tradition in Israel*. London: SCM, 1962.

Congar, Y., 'The Church and Pentecost' in *The Mystery of the Church*. London: Chapman, 1965. 146-204.

Cuming, G.J. *Hippolytus: a text for students*. Bramcote, Notts: Grove Books, 1976.

Daly, R.J., *Christian Sacrifice*. Washington: Catholic University of America Press. 1978.

Eco, U., *Semiotics and the Philosophy of Language*. Bloomington: Indiana Uni Press, 1986.

Feeley-Harnik, G., *The Lord's Table. Eucharist and Passover in Early Christianity*. Philadephia: University of Pennsylvania Press, 1981.

Fink, P., 'Perceiving the Presence of Christ'. *Worship* 58, 1984, 1, 17-29.

Fink, P., 'Living the Sacrifice of Christ'. *Worship* 59, 1985, 2, 133-48.

Fink P., 'The Challenge of God's Koinonia'. *Worship* 59, 1985, 5, 386-403.

Fink P., 'The Significance of Meal in Christianity' in *Worship: Praying the Sacraments*, Washington: Pastoral Press, 1991, 63-80.

Gerken, A., 'Historical Background in the New Direction in Eucharistic Theology'. *Theology Digest*, 25, 1977, 46-53.

Guthrie, H.H. *Theology as Thanksgiving*. New York: The Seabury Press, 1981.

Jaubert, A., *The Date of the Last Supper*. New York: Alba House, 1965.

Jeremias, J., *The Eucharistic Words of Jesus*. London: SCM, 1966.

Kaspar, W., 'The Unity and Multiplicity of Aspects of the Eucharist'. *Communio* 12, 1986, 115-38.

Kilmartin, E., 'The Catholic Tradition in Eucharistic Theology: Towards the Third Millenium'. *Theological Studies*, 55, 1994, 3, 405-57.

Kilmartin, E., *The Eucharist in the Primitive Church*. Englewood Cliffs, N.J.: Prentice Hall, 1965.

Ledogar, R., 'The Eucharistic Prayer and the Gifts over which it is Spoken'. *Worship* 41, 1967, 6, 578-96.

Legrand, H.M., 'The Presidency of the Eucharist according to the Ancient Tradition.' *Worship* 53, 5 (1979) 413-431.

Ligier, L., From the Last Supper to the Eucharist in (ed) L Sheppard, *The New Liturgy*. London: DLT, 1970. 113-150.

Marshall, I.H., *Last Supper and Lord's Supper*. Exeter: The Paternoster Press, 1980.

Mazza, E., *Mystagogy (A Theology of Liturgy in the Patristic Age)*. New York: Pueblo, 1989.

Osborne, K., 'Eucharistic Theology Today'. *Worship* 61, 1987, 2, 98-125

Power, D.N., Irenaeus of Lyons on Baptism and Eucharist. *Alcuin/Grow. Liturgical Study* 18. Bramcote, Notts, 1991.

Power, D.N., *Ministers of Christ and his Church*. London: Geoffrey Chapman, 1969.

Robinson, J.A.T., *The Body* London: SCM, 1952.

Rordorf, W. (& Others), *The Eucharist of the Early Christians*. New York: Pueblo, 1978.

Sloyan, G.S., Jewish Ritual in the First Century C E and Christian Sacramental Behaviour. *Bib Th Bull 15, 3* (1985) 98-103.

Talley, T., The Eucharistic Prayer of the Ancient Church according to Recent Research: Results and Reflections. *St Lit* 11 (1976) 138-158.

Talley, T., The Literary Structure of the Eucharist Prayer. *Worship* 58, 5 (1984) 404-420.

Westermann, C., The Re-presentation of History in the Psalms. in *Praise and Lament in the Psalms*. Atlanta: John Knox Press. 1981.